The Cry

How God Responds to the Crisis of Identity, Emotional Wellness, and Sexuality of Generation Alpha

Dr. Tamara Denis-Lewis

The Cry
How God Responds to the Crisis of Identity, Emotional Wellness, and Sexuality of Generation Alpha

DENIS-LEWIS, DR. TAMARA, Author
THE CRY
DR. TAMARA DENIS-LEWIS

INTO HIM, LLC

Published by:
ELITE ONLINE PUBLISHING
63 East 11400 South, Suite #230
Sandy, UT 84070
EliteOnlinePublishing.com

ISBN: 978-1-971310-20-6 (eBook)
ISBN: 978-1-971310-21-3 (Paperback)

REL012030
FAM034000
REL109030
Edited by Elizabeth Maynard Charle

CONTENTS

The ultimate test of a society is the kind of world it leaves to its children.

–Dietrich Bonhoeffer

Free Gift - Download the free printable
gift by scanning the QR below.

IntoHim.org/gift

A NOTE OF GRATITUDE

There are a few people without whose support this book would not be possible.

I would like to thank my husband, John Lewis, who has supported every aspect of this book and provided me with the freedom to launch all my dreams and visions. Thank you for your abundance of patience, unconditional love, and unwavering sacrifice toward me and our children.

To our children, Israel and Jewel — thank you for being such amazing kids. May you outdo us in your love for our precious Lord and Savior, Jesus Christ, all the days of your lives.

Thanks to my mom, Marie Jean Baptiste, for being such a great example of what it means to love, pray, and serve her enemies like they are friends. Thank you for persevering through a challenging journey. You are the BEST mom ever. Que Dieu te bénisse.

To my cousin, sister, and best friend, Peggy Jean Baptist-Fletcher — thank you for your love and unwavering presence throughout this journey.

To my precious mentor, friend, and sister in Christ, who loved me unconditionally, prayed for me, listened to my cries, and burned the midnight oil with me as I labored to write this book — thank you, Angela Smith of Norfolk, Virginia.

To the extended part of our family, Ms. Melissa Bryant, for loving our family like your own and for all the years you were there for our children. Only heaven can thank you enough.

Thank you, Diane Hallman, for your endless and fervent prayers over me and my family, and for all the encouragement you sent throughout so much of this journey.

ACKNOWLEDGEMENTS

To my brother Brad Denis, I love you. To my oldest and late brother, Martin H. Denis — thank you for looking over us. Until we meet again.

Camara Manon Denis, Camaro Denis, Merline Barrington-Denis, Alexander Denis, Larissa Denis-Utelmy, Lance Denis — may we pass a godly legacy to the generation that follows us.

To my nephews Zion, Tyler, Marcus, Liam Denis, and Levi Barrington — may you grow to be great men and godly leaders in your homes.

To my nieces Kadyn, Elliana, Mikayla Denis, Isabelle Barrington, and Layla Utelmy — may you exemplify the essence of godly beauty in Christ.

To my uncle, aunts, elders, and cousins who have supported me in love and prayer — I am forever indebted to you for such depth and commitment: Uncle Hervé and Marie José Jeanbaptiste, Melissa Jeanbaptiste, Bevilton and Joanna Morris, Antonine Beaublanc, Janeane Manigant, Sheila Henry, Joselyne Denis, Marjorie Denis, Jempsey Dasque, Yolette Davidson, Leslie Coutard, Dorothy Borno, Doris Dorilas, Magaly Bowen, Chantal Giordani, Sandra Balmir, Berthy Dasque, and Katia and Glenn Xavier, Evans Dasque, Christine Jean Baptiste, Alexandra Jean Baptiste, Gredele Jean Baptiste, Betty Jean Baptiste, Ariel Xavier.

To my KLAMP Community — Sarah King, the Lewis Family, Dede Adetutu, Monica Mouer, Harriet Mouer, and Nicki Powers: your love is a treasure. Thank you for being like family.

Principals Dr. Theresa Jackson, Doris Land, Brenda Shepherd, Dr. Dawn Lawrence, Dr. Sharon Phillips, Angela Grant, and Brenda Mills — thank you for the honor and privilege of serving children under your leadership.

BLAST *(Building Leaders, Authors, Speakers and Teachers)* Leader Shannon Ethridge — thank you for all your support and encouragement in sharing the stories of my teaching journey. You have guided me through so many seasons. You are such an original.

Writing Tribe Trudy Seward, Donna Spencer, Dena Johnson, and Sharon Williams — thank you for being such an amazing writing tribe as we launched our visions together with love and laughter.

Mentors Dr. Bill Cashion, Dr. Larry McDonald, Angela Smith, Theda Okona, Pastor Wanda Adkins, Pastor Cheryl Mintor, Ministers Carolyn and Larry Ward, and Diane Hallman.

Friends Kathleen St. Fleur, Melba Peterson, Xaviera Brown, Dr. Stephanie Gray, Bonnie McDaniels, Toni Johnson, Sarah Johnson, Shilisa Daniels, Allycia Brown, Mona Wesley, Latoya Phelps, and Angela Smith — thank you for being there through thick and thin. I love you.

Editors Thank you Amy Miller for your edits. Thank you to my major editor, Elizabeth Maynard Charle, for doing a splendid job in polishing up my work.

PREFACE

"Stand at the crossroads and look; ask for the ancient paths, ask where the good way is, and walk in it, and you will find rest for your souls."

Jeremiah 6:16

What happens to a generation when they stop hearing God's voice? More importantly, what happens when no one notices they've stopped listening? This question has followed me for more than thirty years. I've heard that question echo in my classroom, in my dreams, and in the depths of my prayers. It became what I now call "The Cry." It is the sound of God's heart for our children, and their aching cry back to Him.

I was that teacher who spent decades in tough inner-city classrooms, and my students consistently outperformed what the district thought was academically possible. While the accolades, awards, and high standardized scores for my students came, none of that was the spark for my initial cry and the writing of this book. All of it came after The Cry first found me in a very unusual place.

The journey began with a cry of my own. There were yearnings and groans that could not be fully expressed with words, and they were cries that kept me up at night. While I wasn't so sure how to express what I needed, I was confident that I wanted to know God personally. I had read the Bible from back to cover several times, yet there was a gap between what I read and what I needed from God. Immersing myself in God's world led to many encounters with Him. My search for God landed me on a path that traced back to the root and foundation of my own youth.

God dealt with the child in me and journeyed me through what He wanted every child to know about Him. I had just started my career as a teacher in inner-city public schools. The more I engaged with children from broken lives, the more my lens became deeply sensitive to their need for God and my need as a child of God. My journey as a teacher was filled with visiting children who lived in projects, doing their laundry, washing their hair, getting to know their families, and taking carloads of them to church on the weekends.

Within the classroom, I wanted to infuse ways that they could find hope in many hopeless circumstances. My heart was broken over their lives and their needs. Whenever I would look into their eyes, I would be reminded of me, and I wanted more than anything to give them what they so greatly yearned for—God.

As I prayed and cried out to God, He would give me unusual dreams of how to teach them. He would give me jingles, songs, ways to break the lessons down, and things to do that would let them know how deeply they were loved by me and how deeply they were loved by God.

God's voice in my ear made me a very unusual teacher. I did things that did not fit the curriculum or mimic what my peers were doing in their classrooms. Some teachers loved and accepted me, and others did not. I was too engaged with my students to care.

God would wake me up in the night and call out my students by name only to tell me how I was to explain the lesson the next day so that the child would understand it. None of what I did was in the lesson plan. This made me a misfit, yet I had some leaders who gave me freedom to do what I did as they knew the outcome would always prove true on state standardized tests. My favorite principal simply smiled, shut the door, and allowed me to do what I did best, be the teacher God called me to be.

While I'd love to say that all of these experiences drew me to that unusual place in which I found myself, this wasn't the case.

The way that journey started was not pretty. It wasn't some holy, peaceful moment with gentle music playing in the background. It began in darkness. I was in so much pain. I would crawl under my bed at night and sleep there because somehow it felt safer than the world around me. I thought maybe if I could get low enough, hide deep enough, nobody, not even God, would see how broken I was, yet He did.

That's where He found me ... under my bed. I remember it as clear as if it happened yesterday. I was lying there, numb, tired, and distraught; then suddenly, I wasn't alone.

Jesus appeared under my bed where I lay quietly. I had never seen Jesus before, but the moment I saw Him, I knew it was Him. His presence didn't feel like judgment, it felt like ... warmth. Like love. Like a mother holding her baby and saying, "I've got you."

At the time, I didn't even have the energy to be amazed. I just remember feeling His arms around me with the kind of comfort that goes deeper than words.

I didn't know back then that God could mother you, but He did that night. Later, I came across the verse in Isaiah 66:13 that says, "*As a mother comforts her child, so will I comfort you.*" When I read that, it just hit me: that's what I experienced. That's what He was doing.

That moment changed me. It didn't fix everything overnight, but it planted something inside me. It was like He whispered, "You're not lost. I'm still here." Looking back, that was the start of everything.

During that season, I went through a lot of powerful experiences: visions, dreams, visitations, and moments that were so vivid I didn't know if I was awake or asleep.

There was one visit from Christ that's never left me. Jesus took me on a long, dusty road. Even though I was a grown adult, during Christ's visit, I was a little girl, maybe eight or nine years old, walking hand-in-hand with Him. My clothes were ragged and dirty, but He was leading me somewhere.

We walked for what felt like miles until I saw a palace in the distance. It was beautiful, shining in the light that was just starting to break through the dawn. When we reached it, a servant met us at the door. Jesus didn't say anything. He just smiled, and then suddenly, He was gone. The servant took me inside and helped me change my clothes. She bathed me, dressed me in a royal gown fitting for a girl. For a moment, I just sat there looking at myself, not used to seeing that reflection in the mirror.

But then a bell rang, loud and sharp, and the servant rushed back in saying it was time to change again into the next royal dress. I didn't want to. I liked what I had on, and honestly, it felt good. It finally felt *me.* But she insisted. Each hour, the bell rang, she came back with new garments, and every time, I argued. Until finally Jesus appeared again and said, "Tamara, it is time to change your apparel. In My kingdom, My greatest design is change."

That statement struck me. I didn't know then that He was teaching me something that would define my whole life and that of the youth I would come to work with. That change, even painful, uncomfortable change, is part of God's design. That's how He grows us and He wants to impart this early on to our youth.

God modeled to me how change happens through the ancient biblical practices that He would engage in with me during my time with Him. During various dreams and visitations, he showed me how to impart what kids were crying out for the most. None of these practices provide perfection but they are pathways that lead to connection with Christ through the facilitation of godly leaders.

If you are an adult who in any capacity engages with youth, God is asking you to be a steward and allow for opportunities for constant transformation, spiritual transformation. He has shown me that in His kingdom, the greatest design is still change.

In those early years of teaching in inner-city public schools, I stepped into classrooms that felt like a different world. Some of my students came from homes where both parents were in prison. Some were being raised by grandparents or by no one at all. Some were quiet and withdrawn; others carried anger that could fill a room. But all of them, every single one, had a story. And underneath those layers of toughness and survival, I could feel their cries too.

One of many stories in my journey as a teacher is that of Jathan Wilford. Jathan Wilford is a student whose life has been etched in the crevices of my heart to this day.

His mother was a prostitute, and the one male figure in his life was his uncle, a drug addict, who would occasionally show up in my classroom to roughen up Jathan whenever he misbehaved. Jathan came into my third-grade class on a kindergarten reading level. I used all my youthful energy at the time to work beyond school hours to build him up to a third-grade reading level. At the end of the school year, we celebrated his success on the state standardized test. Yet the more I got to know Jathan, the more

I was moved with compassion for more than what he needed academically.

Little by little I dove into his world of brokenness and poverty. I asked myself how could a child in his circumstance have any glimpse of God? Who would ever bring him to church or even crack open the Bible and share the truth with him? The answers were daunting. So, I sought ways on how I could bring heaven to him. With regular close walks and talks at recess, laughter during small groups, and love between lessons, Jathan experienced the love Christ gave to His disciples.

Jathan went on to middle and then high school. I often wondered what became of Jathan. Years later I noticed a tall slim young man in the corridor of my classroom door. He had gold teeth and a thick gold chain that kept me from putting the puzzle pieces together and notice the younger version of Jathan through this young man's eyes. When I finally recognized him, I broke down with tears of joy. He managed to remind me of the long walks we took during recess as I told him of the One who loved him most. We laughed and chatted about the funny experiences we shared. Jathan so valued these practices we shared in the third grade that he brought them back to my memory and reminded me that he did have a glimpse of God through these practices. Through it all I knew Jathan was still enduring a hard life.

Before he left, I felt compelled to remind him that at any point of need he could cry out the name of Jesus and God would respond immediately with nothing less than abundant love and forgiveness. Following that visit from him, I later learned that Jathan was tragically gunned down. My last words to him echoed in my own heart with all hope that he remembered the precious practices we shared as I told him about Christ. Those practices were bridges he could use even when the hopes of visiting a church or even reading a Bible were grim. Those practices are what Christ's disciples held onto as Jesus ascended back to heaven. Those practices are what the Generation Alpha can experience as they journey through a life that leaves them spiritually malnourished.

Over time, I realized that God had placed me in inner-city public schools for a reason. My students became ministry, even when I couldn't talk about God openly. He was teaching me to see the spiritual side of what was happening in their lives; to look beyond the surface, beyond the behavior, and hear the pain underneath.

I've been teaching for over thirty years now. That's three decades of watching kids grow up in a world that keeps getting louder and more confusing. I've seen their struggles change shape but not disappear. They're battling things most adults can barely handle. We're talking anxiety, loneliness, identity confusion, depression, and addiction. And the truth is, they're crying out for something real.

God started showing me that the same love that met me under that bed is reaching out to them. Generation Alpha, is not too young to know Him. They're not too young to have face-to-face encounters with Him. They're just surrounded by so much noise that it's hard for them to hear His voice. The world tells them who to be, what to believe, what to post, and what to love, and it's all happening before they even know who they are. But I believe God is still calling them.

During my doctoral studies, I started researching what I saw daily in my classroom and what I experienced in dreams. I studied the spiritual and psychological development of children. And what I found confirmed what I had been feeling all along: that this generation is spiritually hungry. They are looking for truth, even when they don't have the words for it.

Sometimes, I'd leave school so heavy. I'd sit in my car and cry because I wanted to pray for them but couldn't do it in the classroom.

I'd think about the student who told me she didn't want to live anymore, or the one who said he couldn't stop watching things that were destroying his mind. And I'd think, "Lord, they need You."

The world keeps calling them "Generation Alpha." But to me, they're the *crying* generation: crying out for love, purpose, identity, and truth. Not only do their cries land in the ears of a God who cares, but He, too, is crying for their return to Him. His cry is for wholeness, for healing, for them to come back home to Him. More than being the Alpha or crying generation, they may also be the Omega generation; the generation that may be here to see the return of the Lord. We must be leaders that prepare them for the greatest season the church and the world have ever seen.

I think about what Jesus said in that dream: *In My kingdom, My greatest design is change.* I believe He's calling this generation to transformation, to move from brokenness into wholeness, from confusion into clarity, from fear into love. And He's calling us, parents, teachers, pastors, and mentors, to be part of that process.

I remember asking God once, "Why me?" Why did He trust me with this message? Why did He give me these dreams, these encounters? And He said, "Because you cried too." I think that's the link ... His cry meets ours, and that's where purpose is born.

One day, I know I'll stand before Him, and He'll ask, "Tamara, what did you do with what I gave you? What did you do with the revelations, the dreams, and the teaching?" I want to be able to say I didn't keep quiet. That I told it all. That I tried my best to pass it on, not just to teachers or preachers, but to anyone who loves a child.

So that's what *The Cry* is. It's my story: the story of a teacher, a mother, and a dreamer. It's also the cry of all the many children who have crossed my path in the classroom setting. But more than that, it's God's response to their cries as the most loving Father. It's

His heart for this generation and what He's saying to all of us who care for them. It's about the ancient ways He still uses to reach His children and how those ways can still work now, in a world that thinks it's outgrown Him.

If you're a parent, a grandparent, a pastor, a youth leader, a teacher, or just someone who loves the next generation, this book is for you. Because God is still crying out for His children. And He's asking us to cry with Him, to listen, to lead, and to love them back home.

PART I

THE PROBLEM

Section Preview

Only when we truly understand the problem can we fully appreciate why they need an answer … and why that answer must be Jesus.

This section is where the journey begins. It's where I share what I have seen with my own eyes and felt in my spirit while walking alongside Generation Alpha—as a teacher, a mother, and a follower of Jesus Christ.

These are not distant theories. These are real moments, real conversations, real struggles, and real questions coming from children who are growing up in a world far louder, faster, and more confusing than any generation before them.

As I share these real moments and struggles, I also emphasize the vital role of parents, grandparents, relatives, and spiritual leaders. I urge them to reclaim and steward their God-given position with intentionality for the sake of their children.

During my three-decade journey, I have had many prophetic dreams, visitations, and impressions God has given me about this generation, to bring awareness of God's insight. Each chapter will begin with these encounters.

When we're keen on what our children are facing beneath the surface—identity confusion, mental battles, sexual pressure, and spiritual emptiness—we can no longer stay passive or assume they'll "just figure it out."

This section is meant to help you see them differently. To hear what they are not always able to say out loud. To feel the urgency behind their questions and understand why their cry for truth, safety, and belonging cannot be ignored. It will also show you how you can play a vital role in leading them into a real, face-to-face relationship with God, one that is intimate and alive with His power in their lives.

If you want to:

- Learn about the questions ruminating in the minds of Generation Alpha, **read on.**
- Learn of the identity, mental, and sexual cries of Generation Alpha, **read on.**
- Read the prophetic dreams and visions given to me by the Lord about the Generation Alpha, **read on.**
- Learn how parents, grandparents, godly relatives, and youth pastors can take back their authority, **read on.**

My Dream...

Pruning Through the Spiritual Diet of Our Youth

Surrounded by babies, I found myself in an orphanage. I watched as many of the babies were fed, and they were healthy, content, and at peace.

On the other hand, the baby in my arms had not been fed milk.

As I frantically searched for a bottle of milk to calm the baby's piercing cries, I found several bottles filled with a white liquid. Just as I felt a sense of relief for both the baby and myself, I instinctively knew that the bottles, though they looked like milk, were poisonous.

As I continued searching for real milk to feed the baby, she began to voraciously suck on objects, as if trying to extract milk from anything within reach. The baby sucked on the edge of the counter, my finger, and everything she could put her mouth on.

Like this baby, Generation Alpha is craving the milk of who God is, and they are sucking on anything that resembles God or promises even temporary relief for their spiritual hunger pangs.

At times, what they latch onto is treacherous to their souls, grievous to their spirits, and stunting to their spiritual development.

When spiritual leaders fail to discern the appropriate spiritual nourishment for the youth in their lives, what they consume can later prove to be poisonous.

As both a teacher and parent, my heart breaks by the realities I witness the youngest part of our population facing. I am constantly before God in prayer, asking Him to give me discerning eyes to truly hear and understand their cries.

Chapter 1

Guardians at the Gates

The cries of babies are often spoken in articulations that modern languages cannot understand until they are able to verbalize thoughts into language. Yet even young children who are able to speak struggle to clearly say what may be ruminating in their hearts and minds. It is the mature adult, the deeply discerning adult, who must reach deeper to translate what words may not be saying.

> Joshua was a very involved third grader in school. He was part of the basketball team, the book club, and volunteered periodically in the community. His grades were decent, and he went to church with his family every Sunday. During whatever free time he had, he played video games and chatted with friends on social media. On the surface, Joshua appeared to be living a healthy, well-balanced life, but something deeper was quietly unfolding beneath all the activities he was involved in. Late in his second-grade year, he was on social media when a video of a teen popped up that pulled him in. The teen boy went into detail about his struggle with mental anxiety and how he wanted to kill himself by taking pills and leaving a letter for his parents. Joshua could not fully understand the

> depth of the teen's pain, yet the video planted an image in his mind that never left him.
>
> In the fall of Joshua's third-grade year, another image popped up on his screen. No matter how much his parents added protective controls periodically, unusual things would pop up, almost seemingly grabbing him by the neck. This pop-up was of two men engaging in sexual activity. In Joshua's young mind, he thought the image was disgusting, but again, he was now trapped with these images playing in his mind, forming him while everyone around him thought he was okay.
>
> Joshua would come to ache and cry inside with the images that continued to play in his heart, soul, and emotions as culture further sealed the deal. As we may be surrounded by seemingly spiritually healthy youth, it takes a keen and intentional heart and mind to dig deeper and ensure that youth are fully equipped with the tools they need to overcome the world's pressures. During Joshua's developmental stage of curiosity, discovery, and knowledge, he needed this type of constant spiritual guidance, especially to overcome the challenges brought on by social media alone.

Sadly, research shows that Generation Alpha has the highest rate of anxiety and struggles with identity and sexual confusion. They are the first generation that has no idea what life without technology looks like, the first generation that is technologically connected but socially isolated, and the first generation born with laws that support options for their gender.

Generation Alpha, born between 2010 and 2024, is one of our youngest generations alive today. They are at a pivotal stage in which the brain begins to establish beliefs around identity, anchor sources for mental wellness, and develop a sense of sexuality. In light of how this stage translates into spiritual development, spiritual leaders must take note and guide them accordingly. This guidance is known as apprenticeship, a process that allows youth to understand why their faith matters, to immerse themselves in learning, and to freely discover truth for themselves.

As good parents and guardians, it is seamless for us to provide the essential physical needs for our children. If they need food, clothes, or shelter, we instinctively know what to do. We provide and do whatever it takes to get the job done. Even when our children desire non-essentials, we are often ready to sacrifice everything to fulfill even a temporary level of happiness.

Likewise, as godly parents, relatives, and spiritual guardians, we have been honored with the position of stewarding our children's spiritual growth and development. Yet, if we are not intentional in the spiritual aspect of our children's lives, the enemy can begin brewing a party that will not end well as they grow older.

Our children's spirit is where God is invited and where He dwells. It is where they are formed according to God's holy Word, cultivated into His likeness, and protected by unseen darkness and forces that are against the will of God for their lives.

Even while consistently bringing inner-city students to high achievements in standardized state tests over my thirty years as a teacher, I learned that my students were not standards. They were more than that ... they are spiritual beings.

My heart would grieve at watching their hungry spirits crying for more than just a high score or number, and a mundane schedule. They were made to thrive, knowing God loves them and has a great purpose for them to fulfill.

In the same way that King David (in the Bible) tended sheep as a boy, God tends to children through leaders like you, me, and other valuable godly individuals. He keeps a keen eye over their spiritual health. He watches over them even while they sleep. He commands the wolves to go away from them when they want to devour them. He rescues them from danger. He knows them by name. He cleans them up when they get dirty and provides all manner of grace for their well-being. He even carries them on His shoulder so that they can more closely hear His voice.

Looking back at Joshua's story, the young boy who was repeatedly exposed to inappropriate content online, I paused and wondered who is tending his spirit? Who has asked him questions about possible things that have made him uncomfortable on social media? Many parents do a great job of providing for and overseeing the physical well-being of their children, yet more times than not, our children are spiritually malnourished when it comes to the condition of their spirits.

A child who has been trained to involve Christ in all they do will share when something isn't right. A child who is taught to be sensitive to the Spirit of God will not allow abuse or inappropriate pop-ups to marinate inside them. They will not allow anything that does not sit well inside them to remain without telling a trusted adult.

Even though I taught this to my own children in more ways than one, I have to admit something. There were times when I heard the spiritual cries of my children and recognized them. And there were times when I completely missed them. Looking back, I can see moments when they were signaling something deeper, and I did not fully grasp it.

One particular incident still stands out to me.

I remember one incident as clear as day. My son was in the fourth grade and continued to tell me how much he hated school. Gifted in writing and speaking, he had entered a contest where he had to write about his favorite hero. My son wrote about Jesus being his hero, healer, and best friend only to have the teacher take his paper, crumble it, and ask him to respect other people's faith by never saying the name of Jesus again. One morning as we prepared to go to school, my son flopped on the couch and cried, saying, "Mom, I cannot do it anymore." I knew then that we had to make a change, one that would require a sacrifice taking us away from our educational convenience. We shopped around until we found a school that aligned with what we believed and one that would cultivate both of our children's gifts and abilities.

After shifting schools, both my son and daughter thrived for many years. They were both being spiritually fed and academically challenged. This continued for our daughter but as the high school years approached, there was another cry from my son. This time I ignored it. It would have been inconvenient to find yet another school that would meet his needs. He was at a place where he had more questions, more needs, and more depth. Even though the school they attended was an academically rigorous school with consistent godly leaders that taught well, my son's spiritual hunger was what God had assigned me to be attentive to and not any particular school.

He successfully graduated but shared that he had needed something more. My daughter, on the other hand, received the spiritual nourishment that she needed while my son's spiritual hunger went ignored. Our children's spiritual cries vary from one child to the other, but what's important is that they feel the freedom to share their cries and that their cries are heard and validated. We never want them to grow silent because they feel as if they are not heard.

I ended up repenting to God and to my son. Yet the greatest part of this story was one of the many biblical practices woven into our family culture. My son and I used a practice from the time he was a young boy that allowed him to scaffold his cry in more detail through writing. We had a notebook where he would journal what was on his mind, then turn it in to me. I would then read it, acknowledging his thoughts and then share mine. This fostered the flow of expression, reasoning, forgiveness, and most importantly, healing.

Even when parents miss the cries of their children, having practices in place will help to clean up the messy spills we make from time to time.

Our children are born with the tool of letting out their cries in many ways according to their developmental age and when they release their tears, we are called to hear God's voice and respond accordingly.

While writing was the practice we incorporated with my son, the practice used with my daughter was different. Her need was quality time and most of the time this meant a long drive that included breaking bread at Chic Fil-A. After eating her favorite snack, all the things that weighed heavily on her heart would come pouring out. I would quietly listen and later appropriately respond.

The freedom to release discomfort is the response we want our children to have. They must be aware that there is a trustworthy and godly believer they can run to and share whatever darkness may be disturbing their inner peace.

This is where godly parents and spiritual leaders must begin to take authority over both their own spiritual health and the intentional tending of their children's spiritual journey.

The Voice of God in Their Spiritual Ears

The enemy of our souls will wage wars against our seed, and we may not be aware of the battles they face. This happened to my brothers and me during our childhood. As a child of Haitian immigrant parents, I remember how my older brother and I endured significant bullying because we were not English speakers, the way we dressed, our accents, and all the things that made us different.

One day, my older brother came home upset about yet another fight he had gotten into because of one of the bullies. My father happened to be home to greet my brother after school. After long minutes of patiently listening to the dramatic tale my brother shared, my father firmly explained that in our family, we do not lose fights.

The next thing I saw was my dad putting on his jacket while having my brother do the same. My father shared that they were going to find the bully and that my brother would beat him up while my father watched him win.

They went back to the school grounds, found the boy, and my father coached my brother as my brother beat up the boy who had so terribly bullied him for all those years.

While I certainly do not advocate having children take situations like bullying into their own hands, it is important that we coach our children into becoming spiritual champions over the battles that wage war against their spiritual lives. The enemy of their souls is fully intent on stealing, killing, and destroying them. We must provide our children with tools of empowerment to take down the powers of darkness that attempt to take over their souls and spirits. No child of God should be overtaken by this enemy called Satan, because no child of God is set up to lose a fight.

As I grew older and it was time for me to start school, the same pattern of bullying began. As a quiet-natured child and, at times, profoundly timid, I struggled to stand up for myself. The voice of my father would run through my mind, and on one particular bullying occasion, my father's voice was louder than ever. My tiny frame took down the giant enemy of my soul, even though I did it while crying. And from that point on until finishing school, I never lost a battle.

Unfortunately, today our children face bigger wars than what my brother and I faced. They're facing social media wars, lonely wars, anxiety wars, academic wars, mental wars, and sexual wars. During these wars, our children must have a spiritual voice coaching them on how to win every battle.

God's voice must be the loudest one our children hear when they face challenges. Sadly, Generation Alpha is facing things that most adults cannot handle; therefore, their spiritual discernment and response must be taught at a higher level in order to combat what they may face.

The Role of Spiritual Apprenticeship for Youth

What are some of the tools of empowerment that we can equip our children with? Many of these tools can be found in the way God allowed Jesus to form His relationship with Him.

Leading today's youth into a lasting faith requires a model of spiritual discipleship often referred to as apprenticeship. Apprenticeship was the educational model that Jesus' childhood exemplified. From His Bar Mitzvah to His young adult years, Jesus was trained as a spiritual leader under the apprenticeship model. Our children can benefit from this model because of the level of curiosity they possess and the stage of learning they are in.

Neuroscientist Dr. Patricia Goldman from Stanford University discovered that between the ages of eight to twelve, children develop their "epistemic framework," their basic system for determining what is true. During this time, they stop accepting information simply because adults say it. They begin asking, "Why?" and "How do you know?" This period in brain development is often referred to by neuroscientists as a cognitive shift. The Bible references Jesus, around this same age, cultivating His faith and conversing with scholars. (Luke 2:41-52)

Instead of the common approach of simply telling children about God, it is imperative that we train children in the way they should go. This means incorporating practices that provide opportunities for Socratic conversations, meditation, and reflection, which are many of the ways Jesus lived and bridged His time on earth with His Father in heaven.

Jesus spent years under the rabbis and spiritual leaders of His day. Moreover, His greatest apprenticeship was with His heavenly Father. Jesus would spend hours meditating and reflecting on who His Father was. Jesus got alone with His Father and at His crucifixion, He asked His Father many questions. Our children must be accompanied by parents or spiritual leaders who will intentionally cultivate their spiritual development in Christ. Godly connections are bridges that help our youth cultivate lasting faith in Christ.

Based on an eight-year longitudinal study of 5,000 adolescents, Harvard epidemiology professors Ying Chen and Tyler VanderWeele concluded[1] that practices such as biblical meditation help youth cope with stress. They state, "Having a shared set of beliefs, practices, and values instilled at an early age arms young people with some of the tools to navigate the pressure chamber of adolescence."

In Josh McGilvian's book *Grandparenting*, Josh shares a story of a young teenage girl struggling with her faith. When her grandmother learns of this, she begins joining the young lady regularly for lunch, walks, and meaningful moments of conversation centered around Scripture and the modeling of her faith.

---

[1] Siniff, John, and Tyler J. VanderWeele. "Don't Let Church Scandals Rob Kids of Faith's Benefits." USA Today, March 21, 2019.

Later, this same young lady expresses that these moments were the catalyst that anchored her faith into something lasting. It was not the Bible activities or being told what to believe; it was the practices that followed, the modeling that was conveyed, and the key questions asked during quality time well spent that made the difference.

A Columbia University study found that positive relationships with parents and other adults during childhood are associated with better mental health in adulthood, regardless of exposure to adverse childhood experiences. For children, an extremely important resilience factor is a warm, nurturing relationship with a parent, caregiver, or other adult, says lead study author Sara VanBronkhorst, MD, voluntary faculty in psychiatry at Columbia University. "Our study demonstrates that children who have one positive, committed adult-child relationship are less likely to experience depression, anxiety, and perceived stress later in life."

God's charge to spiritual leaders over the lives of children is a sacred one. It is not a role where we dictate to children who God is, but one where we lovingly lead youth along a path of discovering who God is through Scripture and the guidance of the Holy Spirit through ancient biblical practices.

Ancient Paths that lead to Lasting Faith

Biblical history chronicles leaders who invested this type of guidance in the lives of young people. Their investment brought about transformation so that when the challenges of life arose, their faith was unmovable.

Is this not the faith every believer in Jesus Christ desires for their child? One that is not dictated, but discovered; that embodies being permeated and not being forced.

In Scripture, Samuel apprenticed under the spiritual leader of his day (1 Sam. 2:8), and he later led an entire nation that rarely heard the voice of God in their time (1 Sam. 3:4–10).

Esther was a young orphan raised by her uncle, Mordecai, who discipled her in the ways of God. In turn, she saved the Jewish people from genocide (Esther 2:7).

King Lemuel listened to the instruction of his mother regarding what to look for in a wife and set an example for future generations (Prov. 31:1–3).

Timothy was also discipled by his mother and grandmother (2 Tim. 1:5–7), and later by the Apostle Paul. He became part of the foundation of the early church found in the Book of Acts, setting the groundwork for future churches (2 Tim. 1:5).

Without youth being placed under the tutelage of godly leaders who passed down biblical practices, few young people would lead as previous generations once did.

Parents, grandparents, aunts, uncles, and spiritual leaders must take back their spiritual authority for the purpose of pointing a generation crying out for God back to Him.

Adults are often the initial audience of God, yet His eternal eyes ultimately rest on the next generation. God is after a legacy, a lineage, and a kingdom that will never end, and children who grow to love Him make this possible, while the leaders in their lives make it impossible for the enemy to destroy them.

Esther's uncle was intentional about visiting her often, assuring that she was fulfilling the call of God. Timothy's mother and grandmother spoke to him regularly to anchor his faith. Paul wrote letters to Timothy, reminding him of the practices that would keep him in the faith. Likewise, we as parents, relatives, and spiritual leaders must stand on the wall as guards over the lives of our children so that we keep the voice of evil from piercing their souls.

Modern-Day Parents Who Take Their Spiritual Authority

A few years ago, as conversations around gender identity intensified in schools across the country, parent January Littlejohn found herself in a dilemma when her thirteen-year-old daughter began spending time with friends who proudly identified as transgender, though they were still early in puberty.

The irony was that all the girls in her daughter's friend group were also transitioning, which is an anomaly. The girls seemed to be following trends based on what they read, saw, and were immersed in, yet the permanency of this would have lifelong consequences that would be irreversible.

Not only was Mrs. Littlejohn's daughter transitioning at this tender age through her dress, attitude, and identity, but Mrs. Littlejohn also discovered that the school her daughter attended was siding with her daughter by keeping things top secret regarding what her daughter would share with them. Her daughter had changed her given name to that of a boy and shifted from using the girls' bathrooms to the boys' bathroom, all while the school officials cheered her on.

While her daughter expressed silent cries, Mrs. Littlejohn felt as if she was losing her power as a parent. She asked her daughter questions like, "When did you begin to feel like you were not a girl?" and "How did you know this is how you should move in this direction?" With all of her daughter's responses not demonstrating a child mature enough to make such abrupt decisions, such as permanently removing her budding breasts, Mrs. Littlejohn, a Christian and professional counselor knew she had to operate in her God given authority before her daughter fell into a trap she could never get out of.

In short, after much prayer and soul-searching, Mrs. Littlejohn sought out a school that would be in alignment with what she believed. This shift was not done abruptly, but with careful wisdom.

She majored in the majors, and the minors would be handled at the right time. Mrs. Littlejohn removed the phones from all of her children so as not to isolate the one child who was going through this challenge. She realized that her daughter was being fed so much misinformation through social media about transitioning that it seemed impossible to have any say in her daughter's life. She also realized that taking away the phone would limit her daughter's interaction with the girls who were pushing how "cool" it was to be transgender at a time when they were not mentally or emotionally mature enough to make such decisions.

She made sure that the administration at the new school was on the same page with her and her husband as it related to gender and identity. Mrs. Littlejohn did not make a big deal about clothing changes immediately, as she knew that once her daughter's social environment changed, it would impact a change in her daughter as well.

After a tough journey of taking back the spiritual authority God gave Mrs. Littlejohn as a mother, her daughter is now a thriving young adult, established in her natural-born gender, and today agrees that she lost a great portion of her childhood through the experience of transitioning when she was not even mature enough to make decisions about her life, let alone her gender.

Many projections hold that the path Generation Alpha is on will create a higher rate of youth turning away from God. Yet this projection is impossible when godly parents, grandparents, relatives, and spiritual leaders stand their ground and take their spiritual authority.

Mrs. Littlejohn used her God-given authority to impact the trajectory of her daughter's life.

As we reflect on the spiritual authority God has entrusted to us over the lives of our children, we must recognize how much our children are counting on us to be keenly aware of their cries, and how much God is counting on us to lead them to a well where they can drink and never thirst again.

Our children's cries are profound, yet often unheard. Their cries have potential future repercussions when not addressed. More than anything, we must be equipped with the spiritual nourishment that will anchor them into an everlasting faith in God. This is a faith we cannot create for them, but one God has prepared for them to unfold for themselves under our guidance.

In this chapter, we have discussed the urgency of parents and spiritual guides taking back their authority. We have also examined the critical learning stage of Generation Alpha and their yearning to learn and discover truth for themselves under the guidance of godly leaders. We explored how, if we are not discerning spiritual guardians, our children can fall prey to traps and poison, and finally, the value that we as parents and guardians hold as it relates to the possible silent cries our children may be experiencing for God.

We must understand our value in these sacred roles, grow intimate with the Word of God, lead our children to discover God, and rise with loud cries, fervent prayers, and keen eyes.

In the next chapter, we will explore the safe places God creates for youth when their souls are yearning, along with real-life examples of everyday parents and guardians who led their children into a lasting faith using the apprenticeship model.

My Dream...

A Safe Place for Hard Questions

It was one of those dreams that doesn't fade when you wake up. I can still see it, clear as if it happened last night.

I was in this dim basement ... it wasn't fancy, or decorated, just ... ordinary. The kind of place that smells a little like dust and memory, where people go to rest from the noise outside. There was this feeling in the air, like something sacred was about to happen, though no one said a word. I remember looking around and seeing children, teenagers, all races. Some looked like they'd grown up in church, others like they'd seen more pain than most adults. But in that room, those differences just ... disappeared. It felt like everyone was being held together by something invisible but very real.

Truth wasn't found in their churches or on the streets; it was here, in this dim little room that somehow felt more like home than either of those places. Jesus was there, not in the way I'd pictured Him, not glowing or distant, but present. You could feel Him, almost like warmth on your skin. He walked among them, meeting them right in the middle of their confusion. The kids asked things adults would probably whisper about, and He didn't flinch. He listened. He answered, not with lectures but with something that settled deep, like truth that knew where it was going.

The world had called them lost kids: too anxious, too angry, too uncertain about who they were. But in that basement, they laughed, they leaned in, and they belonged. I saw Jesus sitting right there with them, cross-legged on the floor, as He was a part of them. With all of His glory He sat with kids with sneakers and jeans. He didn't look like someone in charge. He looked like someone who understood. When He spoke, the room went still. Not out of fear, just that kind of stillness that happens when love walks in and everyone recognizes it.

Then He looked at me, and I swear it felt like He'd been waiting to do that. "Gather them," He said. "It's time for Communion." So, we sat together in a circle, no table, no ceremony, just … us. The light in the room shifted; it got warmer and softer. He broke the bread, lifted the cup, and said those same words I've heard a thousand times, only this time they landed differently: "This is my body, broken for you, do this in remembrance of me. Then He took the cup and said, "This is my blood, poured out for you (The blood of the new covenant)." (Luke 22:19-20)

He went to each child, one by one. They didn't hesitate. They received it like it was something they already knew belonged to them. They understood the close connection between them and the God that was sharing Communion with them. No one was trying to perform or pretend. Watching them, I felt this deep peace, the kind that doesn't have words. That basement, with its cracked walls and scuffed floor, felt like heaven had leaned close enough to touch.

When He finished, Jesus didn't preach. He just stayed there with them, quiet and present. I remember thinking that this was what the Church was always meant to look like. Not polished, not perfect, just people finding a sense of home in His presence.

That was the dream.

Their belonging was Communion. God saw how disconnected we had become, how children and whole nations were drifting, so He allowed His own body to be torn apart, only to raise it again in wholeness. Through that, we were handed this gift of Communion with Him and with one another.

We like to leave Communion at the surface level, the bread and the cup, because it feels easier that way. But what Jesus gave those young people in that basement was something deeper. It was the reminder that God loved them enough to let His own body be broken and restored so they could know wholeness for themselves. God wants us to live out that kind of communion, especially in front of the children who are desperate for sacred spaces like the one in my dream.

Scripture says in 1 Corinthians 11:29-30 that many die prematurely because they don't discern the Lord's body. When young people grow up without closeness to God and His people, they never get to discern that body, and it leads to a slow death of isolation, abandonment, and sometimes even suicide. They're not always dying physically, but they are dying spiritually right in front of us. And the need to belong is so powerful that even the kindest, most well-meaning child can end up in groups that pull them away from everything good they've ever known. Yet God has already prepared a way for them to find their belonging in Him.

When the dream finally faded, the light and the faces and even the sounds slipped away, but that feeling stayed with me. Unity. Peace. Love weaving its way through kids the world usually forgets.

When I woke up, my face was wet with tears. Not tears of sorrow, just this deep, almost overwhelming insight. A hope that whispered there was more for youth everywhere. These weren't tidy Sunday school kids. They were the kids I taught every day, the ones who were tough and tired, brilliant and wounded, all at the same time. In that dream, I had seen what my heart had been aching for: a space where they could meet Jesus without fear or filters.

For over thirty years, I had stood in classrooms full of kids like that. I had tried every method, program, and strategy anyone handed me. But that dream showed me something every curriculum had missed. They didn't need more teaching. They needed belonging—a safe place where the Holy Spirit could move freely among them, where communion wasn't a ritual but a relationship.

Lying there with my pillow soaked and my heart wide open, I felt like God had given me a glimpse of His heart for the young and the unseen. I didn't fully understand what He was asking of me then, but I knew it was something significant. That dream became the steady pulse beneath everything that followed: the teaching, the ministry, and the writing.

Whenever doubt shows up, I go back to that basement. To the laughter. To the warmth. To the moment when heaven felt close enough to breathe.

Chapter 2

Rooted Too Deep to Be Uprooted

The best answers begin with questions. Young children are designed from the onset to ask many questions. Many of their questions demonstrate that they are building neural connections while grasping the world around them. It also shows that they understand that asking questions is the pathway to finding answers. Jesus uses questions to prompt thinking in adults; how much more can questions cultivate the critical thinking skills we desire in children?

In my years as a teacher, it has been common to have children ask many questions during lessons. In more recent years, the types of questions have changed, becoming more profound and even more complex. I hardly ever hear questions like why is the sky blue? Why do people die? Or why do we have to follow rules? Children have a different sphere of curiosities, questions, and foundations that they are eager to build upon.

It was just another ordinary day in class, a simple lesson on how different cultures celebrate holidays around the world. Then, out of nowhere, the room started filling up with these big, heavy questions that you don't really expect kids that young to be wrestling with. After sharing how Jewish people celebrate Hanukkah, Jordan innocently called out, "I think I would like to be a 'Hanukkahn' religion when

I grow up, that sounds like fun," he said with an emphatic smile, as if faith were a costume, you could try on. When we got to Ramadan and the many gods that they pray to, another child shyly whispered, "What is prayer?"

Way in the back of the classroom, Muhammad leaned over with a grimace all over his face, scoffing to Jeremy and saying, "Jesus isn't even real."

I remember rubbing my hand over my forehead as I attempted to calm the storm erupting in my classroom. When did spiritual confusion become this normal for children? When did questions about God, truth, and identity become playground conversations instead of bedtime reflections? Worst, when was there a generation who had never heard of prayer? All faiths pray. That was the moment I realized that Generation Alpha isn't indifferent to faith—they're crying out for clarity, for truth, and for someone to help them make sense of a world that is already shaping their souls.

Questions like these became the norm. Before starting a review game and sorting the students by gender, William adamantly asked, "Why do I have to be a boy just because I was born that way? Doesn't that just mean the doctors assigned that to me?"

The normalcy in his voice showed how common this topic has become among kids his age, yet he was asking a question that most adults can't even really articulate properly without feeling uncomfortable.

The questions that Jordan and William have are welcomed, yet, who is adequately answering these questions in such a way to anchor them in truth?

Questions are a normal means for kids to grow and add to their knowledge but in a setting like public school where most children go to school, teachers are not permitted to even address some of these questions with a yard stick. Children like William and Jordan then depend on their culture and social media to solidify their confusion and misconceptions.

Christ on the other hand, welcomes these questions. More than that, He provides a safe place to clarify confusions without condemnation. This is seen in Luke 16:18 when the disciples attempt to send the children away and Christ calls them back as one of His highest priorities. Jesus invites many but especially children in the following way, "Take my yoke upon you and learn of me for I am gentle and lowly of heart," Matthew 11:29. Jesus assures that no question would offend Him and that He is humble enough to understand curiosities and is a patient teacher prepared to answer all kinds of questions.

The use of ancient biblical practices, through the power of God's Holy Spirit, provides ways for children to learn more about Him. Much time will be spent on this topic in upcoming chapters; but for now, let's continue to sit with where our youngest part of society wrestles and where they seek truth for their future.

On a rainy day, when recess took place inside the classroom rather than outside, I began to randomly pass out art paper for those who wanted to draw. Almost offended, Maya, with crayon in hand, asked, "Why did you give me pink? That's racist!"

Her small face twisted in confusion inaccurately repeating something she had heard. I couldn't help but pause, realizing how deeply culture had already seeped into the lives of my young students.

Finally, there was Liam, who, normally cheerful and easy-going, slammed his head on the desk, kicked it away, and ran to the door, collapsing in tears. Later, I learned that he'd been on the phone the night before, ready to end his life while his eight-year-old peers cheered him on.

These might sound like rare cases, but these are the problems our children are facing today. This is the reality for so many of the kids I teach: anxiety, loneliness, hyper sexualization, and social pressure arising before even double digits.

With all the classroom management and structure that exists in my classroom, nothing could stop the questions that naturally exuded from the hearts and mouths of my students. They wanted answers.

Jordan, Maya, Liam, William ... they're all part of Generation Alpha. They're the first kids raised fully inside the digital age, not just using technology but absorbing it as their native environment. They've never known life without tablets, smart classrooms, TikTok-level attention spans, or the constant pressure to "perform" socially even as children. They are the first generation absorbed with sexual identity and the options that follow. They are also the first generation being raised by the highest level of NONES (None of the Above as it relates to religion). They're growing up faster, exposed earlier, and in many ways carrying weight Gen Z didn't face until much later.

And while the world shifts under their feet, the gap between what they're up against and what we're giving them keeps widening. We don't even realize how quickly that gap grows year after year

In *Faith for Exiles* by David Kinnaman and Mark Matlock, they share, "One crucial aspect of forming a coherent identity in our youth, is exposing youths to a greater range of information and insight about where they come from through a biblical lens."[2] Yet, from the lessons we give, the programs we plan, the youth events we run, they barely 'scratch the surface.

[2] David Kinnaman and Mark Matlock, *Faith for Exiles: 5 Ways for a New Generation to Follow Jesus in Digital Babylon*, Baker Publishing Group, 2019, p. 39 (chapter on forming a resilient identity).

They are like spiritual baby food for adult-sized struggles. Still, we respond with surprise when confusion, despair, and frustration spill over to the youngest age group.

When I hear the kind of questions I hear in classrooms, I immediately think of my dream in that basement. The dream where kids from everywhere, some from Christian homes, some from the streets, and even those from other faiths were together in a place where they could freely ask the questions that they were scared to speak out loud to others.

They brought their confusion, their fears, and the questions no one else would answer. They leaned on Jesus directly, rather than on TikTok, Instagram, or whatever was trending. Christ was their friend and welcomed them in a way that I had never seen in a church, home, or anywhere.

That dream shaped everything I noticed, taught, and prayed over in the weeks that followed. It showed me the gap between what kids get in schools and churches and what they're really looking for: a faith they can hold onto, practices that actually stick, and encounters that change them from the inside out. It is a faith they don't just mimic while they're young out of obedience and leave when their old enough, but one that lasts a lifetime.

Looking through that lens, I saw the bigger story of Generation Alpha: they are a generation stepping into a world full of opportunity, but also full of challenges. Their hunger is real, their questions are urgent, and they need our help and spiritual intervention. They need God. They need Him in a way that is tangible and real. And they need it now. I keep being reminded that the dream was a call: to see them, meet them, and give them the spiritual nourishment they need to shape not just their lives, but become leaders to the generations to come.

The Cry That Cannot Be Silenced

Youth pastors, parents, grandparents, and anyone trying to raise kids in faith must respond to the cries being expressed by our youth. Research shows that the statistics of inner-city children compares closely to that of children who are raised in church. We think our children are safe. But now through exposure to social media, they are exposed to adult material as early as five, eight, and ten years old. In essence, they are reading adult content that even adults shouldn't read.

Are our children a priority when it comes to knowledge and spiritual growth? As we speak, children are holding 3 percent of church budgets when it comes to church planning and investments. They were a low priority in Jesus' day, too, as evidenced by how the disciples sent them away from Jesus. Yet Jesus stopped the behavior of the disciples and called the children back to Him, placing them face to face with Him. They hold low priority in many ways socially, in church, and in state planning as shown through low teacher pay, yet they are 100 percent of the future.

Every time I see a young person walk away from faith—every time I watch brilliant, gifted, sensitive children like Jared choose the world over the church—a piece of my heart breaks.

What gives me hope: that basement dream. In that vision, I saw young people who weren't just attending church, they were encountering Christ. They were not just learning about Communion, they were participating in it with understanding and reverence. They weren't just hearing Bible stories; they were living them out. The youth in that dream understood that Communion was part of their spiritual heritage and that it was part of their identity.

They had a keen understanding that this practice connected them to something bigger than their circumstances, more reliable than their feelings, and stronger than cultural pressures.

The Current Situation

If we want to know where we stand, let's look at what we are offering to our children: simplified lessons, programs that entertain, and events that wow for a day and fade the next.

Only about 2 percent of Christian parents and one in eight youth pastors live out a biblical worldview. Most kids have phones before they are thirteen years old. Most of them can't go more than a few minutes without checking it. Nearly half say they're addicted, and honestly, it is evident. Seventy percent of Gen Z teens report anxiety and depression as a "major problem" among peers[3], like it's just a normal part of growing up now.

What's more alarming is that their religious affiliation is dropping fast. Almost four in ten Gen Z kids now say they don't follow any religion at all[4]: they just check "none" and move on. Even the ones who still check "Christian" on a form? A lot of them don't really know what they believe anymore. They've heard the words but lost the meaning. What's worse is that so many churches and youth programs act like this is fine. Like this slow drift away from truth is something we can fix with pizza nights and motivational talks, but research shows otherwise.

Kids are growing up faster than ever, but not in the way we hoped. By eight, they've already seen sexual content online. By ten or eleven, they're questioning who they are, who they're supposed to love, and what any of it means. These are heavy questions ... adult questions ... but they're being dropped on children who barely know how to spell "identity."

All these patterns are breaking them apart. You can see it in their eyes if you look long enough. The anxiety, the loneliness, that faraway

[3] (Pew Research 2018. 2022)

[4] (Pew Research 2019-2023)

stare kids get when they're exhausted by a world they never asked to navigate are all silent cries that often go ignored. Some of them are already thinking about ending their lives before they've even had a chance to live. Adults focus on the behavior ... the outbursts, the shutdowns, and the phone glued to their palms. What they miss is the ache underneath. Research keeps showing the same pattern in youth who reach dangerous breaking points, even in cases like mass shootings: they feel disconnected, unseen, and cut off from belonging. Christ came to answer that cry, yet the spiritual nourishment that anchors a young soul is almost absent in their daily lives.

The way Generation Alpha kids cry out now reminds me of a documentary on Russian infants raised in understaffed orphanages, where adult contact was almost non-existent. Eventually the babies stopped crying out loud. Not because their needs disappeared, but because repeated abandonment taught them no one was coming. Founded in 1978, the Human Rights Watch (a non-government organization that investigates and reports human rights abuses) reported that the lack of meaningful interaction muted their cries into something internal, almost invisible to adults who didn't know how to look for it. The pain didn't go away; it just folded inward, becoming deeper and more complicated. Later, the Bucharest Project followed those same children and found that this silent form of suffering left long-term marks on their emotional, cognitive, and social development.

It's a hard picture to sit with, yet it mirrors what I see in today's youth. When children go too long without real connection, without love that feels safe and steady, and without any sense of God's nearness in their story, they don't stop hurting—they just stop letting anyone hear their cry.

When Jesus said in Matthew 19:14, "Suffer the little children to come unto me," He wasn't inviting them for some sweet moment of story time on His lap. He wanted them close enough to encounter Him for themselves, to bring their curiosity and wonder without being filtered through adult expectations or religious programming. That same openness is what I've seen again and again in my visitations and dreams. These were children whose hearts hadn't been dulled by ritual, and they weren't performing for church culture but were seeing Jesus plainly, without the veil that so often blurs Him for the rest of us.

What stayed with me from that research on the Russian infants was how their cries didn't stop because they were fine; their cries changed because no one actually responded. That same thing is happening with our children today. When we only offer surface-level answers or sidestep the hard conversations, they feel the difference. They sense when adults are uncomfortable, distracted, or giving them the "safe," watered-down version of the truth. So, their cries shift. They take their questions about identity, sexuality, fear, and mental battles inward, where the wounds grow deeper and quieter. It's not that the pain disappears. It's that it learns to hide.

The Ancient Path and Biblical Practices in Modern Day

God's been preparing young people to stand firm in chaotic times since the beginning of time. God has distinctly communicated His priority toward kids like Generation Alpha. Children have always been part of God's plan to reveal courage and truth when everything else feels like it's falling apart. We see this with young Samuel who lived among people who brought in prostitutes, as well as young David who seemed so ordinary among his brothers. We see it even more with the young Hebrew boys, Shadrach, Meshach, and Abednego, who encountered God so intimately that they were able to outwit the leaders of their time.

Let's take a look at one of those examples in a more modern-day America:

Our country was navigating through an identity crisis. They were in a war on whether they would keep old traditions that oppressed others or move toward what was actually written in the Constitution, which was that "all men are created equal." While crowds of people warred in public, a young girl was being raised through the impact that comes from living out ancient biblical practices. Here is her account:

> As a young, Black girl, Ruby Bridges integrated into her all-white elementary school by wading through a mob of nearly a thousand people threatening to kill her. Still early in his career, Robert Coles offered psychological support for this vulnerable child and her family. When Coles learned that Ruby spoke to the mob, he asked her to share with him her words. Ruby explained that she had been praying the same prayer for the mob for months: "Please, please, God, try to forgive these people because they don't know what they're doing."[5] Ruby was uttering the same prayer that Jesus Himself made when confronted by an angry mob. While Coles initially thought the prayer may have been a rote memorization with little significance for the child, upon probing, he learned that Ruby had a relatively sophisticated understanding of its religious meaning and historical context. In addition, she appropriately applied it to a related situation in her own life. She explained the application of this particular story in the following exchange[6]:

[5] Robert Coles, *The Mind's Fate: A Psychiatrist Looks at His Profession* (1975; repr., Canada: Back Bay Books Little Brown and Company, 1995), 13.

[6] Mona M. Abo-Zena and Allegra Midgette, "Developmental Implications of Children's Early Religious and Spiritual Experiences in Context: A Sociocultural Perspective," *Religions* 10, no. 11 (November 15, 2019): 631, https://doi.org/10.3390/rel10110631.

> "'You know when Jesus was in trouble, there was a big mob there. And they were ready to hurt Him. And that's what He said. And I try to say the same thing.'
>
> And, of course, skeptically, I pushed her and said, 'Well, Ruby, do you always believe that?'
>
> She said, 'No, I don't always believe that, but I try to.'
>
> 'How do you try to?' I asked.
>
> She said, 'I close my eyes and I think of what it must have been like for Him'".[7]

Ruby's response is what spiritual transformation looks like. Ruby wasn't performing faith; she was living it. She was practicing empathy, prayer, reflection, all of it, instinctively. That's the result of apprenticeship. That's what happens when a child's soul is actually trained, not just told what to believe.

In today's society, we mostly teach kids about God and not really how to live with Him. We give them verses to memorize, but not practices that help them process anger, anxiety, or confusion. They don't just need knowledge, they need habits ... the kind of everyday faith that kicks in when the world doesn't make sense.

When I read about Daniel or Joseph in Scripture, I see the same pattern Ruby had. Daniel's strength wasn't just willpower; it was practices, rhythm, and prayer. He had a structure to his faith that held him steady when everything else got stripped away. And Joseph, well, his faith didn't survive betrayal and prison because he was optimistic. It survived because he'd already learned to see God's hand in things he didn't understand. These were young people too.

---

[7] Robert Coles, *The Mind's Fate: A Psychiatrist Looks at His Profession* (1975; repr., Canada: Back Bay Books Little Brown and Company, 1995), 15.

It's important to realize that their wisdom didn't just appear, it was immersed in them.

Ruby's immersion looked different, but the heart of it was the same. It was built in tiny, ordinary moments: bedtime prayers, kitchen table talks, and quiet reflection. Her parents didn't just tell her about Christ; they taught her how to see like Him, how to think like Him, and how to be like Him. This is what gave her the strength to walk through that schoolhouse door.

What strikes me most is how integrated her faith was. It wasn't a thing she turned on for church and off for the rest of her life. It shaped everything: her thoughts, words, and reactions. She prayed not to be noticed by God, but because she genuinely needed connection. She forgave not to be in compliance, but because she observed this in the lives of those around her who were spiritually nourished.

Kids like William, Maya, and Liam don't want adults who've got it all figured out. They just want to see faith that's real, that actually works in the middle of the mess.

Ruby was six, small, surrounded by hostility, and yet she had a lifeline in her faith that let her respond with courage, empathy, and prayer instead of recoil. That same kind of lifeline is possible for the kids I see every day, the ones wrestling with identity, anxiety, and questions their young minds aren't fully equipped to answer. The chaos of their world—the social media storms, the pressure to perform, and the creeping doubt about who they are—doesn't have to define them. Ruby's story shows that even in the middle of fear, a child can encounter God intimately and be strengthened from within.

These kids are not just curious; they are carrying burdens that would overwhelm most adults, yet they can still learn to root their identity, their courage, and their moral clarity in Christ, just like Ruby did. They don't need more surface-level lessons or distractions, they need apprenticeship, lived faith, and daily rhythms that teach them how to navigate their fears and confusion with God at the center. If Ruby's small hands could hold steady against a mob, then these children, guided and nurtured in the right ways, can face the storms of their culture with that same quiet strength and anchored hope.

The Ancient Path Forward

"Stand at the crossroads and look; ask for the ancient paths, ask where the good way is, and walk in it, and you will find rest for your souls" (Jeremiah 6:16).

That verse feels alive like a message directed to our generation. The old road, the one built on practices of prayer, reflection, and encounter, isn't outdated. It's proven. It's where the people of God learned how to live with Him, not just learn about Him. Instead, we've swapped practices that formed souls for programs that fill calendars. We've made things louder, shinier, more "relevant," but somehow emptier.

I've spent years watching young people wrestle with questions that no curriculum can answer. I've seen children break under the weight of loneliness and confusion while the adults around them, well-meaning as they are, rush to distract rather than apprentice. I'll never forget the morning one of my students, a bright little girl named Sharon, looked up during circle time and said she felt lonely. Not angry, not sad ... lonely. And it struck me how deeply our children feel, how spiritually awake they actually are, and how starved they've become for presence, for someone to meet them where their hearts already are. They don't need us to be perfect; they need us to be present enough to guide them toward the One who can hold all their questions.

That's what the ancient path offers: not a formula, but authentic paths that lead them face to face with a living God. All the children did in Matthew 19:14 was go to Him, and what did Jesus do? He welcomed them. That is one example of how simple the ancient paths are. When God told His people to retell the story of the Exodus to their children, He was saying, *don't let the next generation forget who they are or where they came from.* The practices of remembrance, conversation, prayer, and storytelling weren't religious theories, they were how faith became real, how identity was shaped, and how young children were passed the baton of everlasting faith.

Those same practices can anchor this new generation too, even in a culture that moves faster than ever. The truth is that Generation Alpha isn't beyond reach; they're wide open. They just need adults who believe their souls are worth slowing down for.

This is no longer a dream. This is a cry. A cry that rises from inner-city classrooms and suburban Sunday school youth groups alike. A cry that echoes through church hallways and school counselors' offices. A cry that says: "We are thirsty. We are hungry for truth. We've been feeding on poison. We are spiritually malnourished." In response, a cry echoes from heaven asking, "Who will feed my sheep?"

If we return to the old road, the one built on conversation, curiosity, imagination, and communion with God, we'll see kids encounter Him in ways we've almost forgotten are possible. We'll anchor our kids in such a way that they can never be uprooted. Our kids will face culture with a faith that is unshakeable. Ruby Bridges did. Daniel did. Samuel did. These children weren't extraordinary because of their times; they were extraordinary because of their intimacy with God in the middle of their times. If God could meet them there, He can meet our children here.

The ancient path still stands waiting. It always leads home where Christ is.

"The entrance of thy words giveth light."

(Psalm 119:130)

My Dream...

Learning in the Unseen Realm

The first thing I remember was standing in a hallway that didn't belong to any school I'd ever taught in. It was a university corridor, polished floors, high windows, and a liberating vibrance that welcomed depths of truth. But what struck me wasn't the setting, it was the unmistakable sense of belonging, a feeling that I was exactly where I was meant to be. In reality, though, I spent my days teaching third graders to develop early literacy skills while asking them to stop digging their noses as they rushed toward me for a hug.

In my dream, I stood by the door like I always did before class, ready to greet a room full of adults.

But when the door opened, the ones walking in weren't college students or even young adults. They were children. Dozens of them. Some barely eight, others in that in-between stage where childhood and adolescence overlap. Yet they carried themselves with a kind expectancy that didn't match their ages. They were eager to continue the conversations from the previous day, looking to go deeper. They sat in random seats, socially free to chat about what overnight reflections brought to the questions previously discussed.

When I stepped into the room, it was as if something in the air shifted. There was warm but confident chatter. There was vibrancy of expectation to be further fueled. It was not going to be a boring lecture. This was not going to be a session of being told what they should believe. This was not going to be a monologue. It was a dialogue.

They were respected individuals on campus who would share in the discussion of the day. We began delving into Scripture like scholars. Depth, context, history, wars, depression, affairs, jealousy, and even the uncomfortable parts most adults tiptoe around. And they absorbed it. Not passively.

We didn't have a sermon that day. We had a conversation that moved like a river, widening and narrowing as it carried us along with emotional empathy, gut-wrenching laughter, reflective pauses, more questions, surprises, and more. The Scripture became a story that was irresistible. It became their story and a memory they would never let go even if they could.

Hands shot up, not for the sake of participation but because they were growing deeper in love with a God that saw their need. They had more questions. Honest ones. Brave ones. Risky ones. They welcomed freedom to be who they were in order to learn who God was, without the sense of intimidation or fear.

Some asked about the world they were growing up in, about sexuality and culture and the things kids usually whisper about when they think adults aren't listening. Others spoke quietly about the battles in their minds, the kind that keep them awake at night. It wasn't chaotic or heavy. It was open. Safe. Authentic. They treated the Word of God like a compass they trusted, not a rulebook someone forced into their hands.

The tech savviness they had in my regular elementary classes was now transferred into their spiritual lives.

Some of these children had been there longer, and their understanding and revelation of Scripture startled me. They handled passages with the discernment of seasoned believers, building connections across the Bible with the ease of someone who had lived inside its pages. They reminded me of the Bereans, searching and testing and anchoring themselves in truth as if it were breath itself. These were not the "youth group kids" churches love to parade around for special Sundays. They were something older and wiser in spirit, and it showed.

The oddest part was how the adults on campus treated them. Professors, staff, even elders would drift into the doorway, quietly listening, sometimes waiting for a chance to ask these children questions. It wasn't patronizing. It was reverent, as if they recognized something growing among these young ones that the world had forgotten: spiritual clarity untouched by cynicism.

And I stood there watching them, realizing that in this strange university, these children were the true teachers. The spiritual giants. The steady ones. The ones holding a light that even the elders leaned toward.

Chapter 3

From Information to Encounter

I had known Jared since he was young. He was a part of our church family, and I had watched him grow. He had always been the good son—the one who went to church, led prayer at youth groups, and bowed his head before meals. But lately, Jared's prayers felt kind of hollow, almost as if the words were echoes that never really reached his heart. Questions stirred in him, quiet at first, then louder. *Who am I? Why do I feel like this? Do I believe all this stuff about God? How do I fit God into all the things I see in my friends, in my battles and in my culture?*

Jared tried to silence the unrest, hiding behind polite smiles and Sunday sermons. But beneath it all was a battle of questions that no one ever really answered, a loneliness he couldn't shake. These battles gnawed at him during school, in worship services, even at home. His youth pastor talked about God's plan, but it never seemed to include kids like him—kids who didn't fit the mold, who questioned everything.

At home, Jared kept quiet. His parents were kind but firm in their faith. Hard and in-depth questions weren't encouraged, not really. What was encouraged was obedience. And so, the young man learned not to rock the boat. Eventually, though, silence took its toll.

By eighteen, Jared knew he couldn't stay in a place that expected him to deny his questions just to belong.

One cold morning, after graduating high school, with his backpack over his shoulder, he stood at the front door. His mother looked up from her coffee and smiled. "Got everything for your day?"

Jared hesitated, then said, "I'm leaving. I need to find out who I really am. I need to know for myself if the God I have been told about is for me."

His parents didn't understand. His father's voice hardened: "You've been raised better than this." His mother whispered, "Please don't go." But Jared had to. He couldn't just keep performing for approval.

"I'm not who you think I am," he said quietly. "I have to stop pretending."

Jared stepped outside, with leaves beneath his feet. He didn't have all the answers, but for the first time in his life, he had space to ask the questions. And that, somehow, felt like freedom.

In many ways, Jared represents what Barna's research shows, that more and more young people are leaving the church by the time they reach adulthood, often because they never felt free to be their authentic selves while they were trying to develop their faith.

When I think about the children who once filled youth Sunday school classrooms and later became rare visitors as adults, I wonder if many parents quietly assumed that faith could simply be "caught" through proximity, that by going to church every week their children would naturally grow into a living, personal relationship with God.

Yet research suggests that this is not the reality for many Christian homes. Across churches and communities, parents, spiritual leaders, pastors, and youth pastors are all witnessing the same heartbreaking trend, a steady exodus of young adults walking away.

True Enlightenment

Providing kids with faith that lasts a lifetime means leading them the way Jesus led His disciples and closest friends. He didn't run them through memory-verse drills. He talked with them about how God's truth connected to whatever they were experiencing in that moment. When the disciples couldn't catch any fish, Jesus used it as a hands-on learning experience of trust and the calling they'd eventually grow into as fishers of men.

When Martha was rushed and overwhelmed in the kitchen, Mary chose to sit and be still. Jesus gently pointed out that letting go of the stress like Mary did was the better choice. Scenes like these show us what real spiritual apprenticeship looks like today. Our youth need what Jesus offered to those closest to Him.

Jesus took long walks in the field with His disciples breaking laws just to illustrate the freedom they had when they were with Him. He used this time to answer their questions, model how to heal the sick, and more importantly, model the way for them to embody His example. This was not a moment in time but a path to everlasting life in Christ.

What Jesus practiced can be done in our modern age through our youngest generation.

* * *

Some stories refuse to leave you alone, and Willie Myrick's is one of them. It's the kind of story that makes you stop and think, *wait … how did a child walk through something like that and come out steady?*

Unlike Jared, young Willie wasn't raised in a Christian home. His parents were atheists, so by all expectations, he should've grown up with a flimsy sort of faith, if any at all. But his godmother stepped in. Willie came to her raw and unedited with questions, curiosities, and even unbelief about the gospel she lived. His godmother gave him the freedom to investigate with long walks joined by conversations, questions, and profound answers rooted in biblical stories and even her own spiritual journey. She didn't preach at him. She didn't sit him down with worksheets or flashcards about God. She just lived her faith in front of him and brought him along with her. Real conversations. Real modeling. Real questions. Real Scripture. Little by little, she gave him a faith that wasn't exactly memorized but lived.

Then came the day everything she built in him was put to the test. It wasn't a memory verse test; it was time for analysis and more importantly application.

Willie was outside playing with his dog, just minding his business, when a stranger snatched him and drove off. Hours passed. The dynamics of Willie's story made headline news. The man planned to harm him in unimaginable ways. This should have been the beginning of a tragic headline. Instead, it became something no one saw coming. Willie sat there in the back seat of the kidnapper's car and started connecting to the God he had been trained to know is available to him whenever he needed Him. He started singing a praise song ... over and over .... Willie learned the power of worship and was immersed in what it meant to persevere in it without being distracted. Willie wearied the kidnapper's ear so much so that the kidnapper kept asking him to stop. Willie found security and safety in singing familiar songs he was used to singing around the house, with his dog and in his daily life. No one was going to take the apprenticeship that had been rooted in his foundation of faith. Instead, it was the kidnapper who would come to such a high level of frustration that he stopped the car and begged him to get out. Somehow, this child walked away without the mental collapse everyone expected. No trauma profile. No anxiety diagnosis. No lifelong shadow.

The contrast with our youth in general is almost painful. Our kids aren't being kidnapped every day, but they are falling apart under pressures that shouldn't break them. A rude comment at school. A forgotten homework assignment. An unlike on social media. A shift in friendship. The smallest thing can spiral them. Anxiety plans and mental-health referrals fill classrooms faster than pencils disappear. Something is off, and we all see it.

So, what did Willie have that Jared and the average child today doesn't?

The same thing Ruby had. A formation that was deeper than Sunday school lessons, deeper than cute memory verses. Their faith wasn't a performance or a ritual. It was a way of life poured into them through relationship, guidance, and a steady pointing back to Scripture. That kind of depth shapes how a child thinks, how they cope, how they understand themselves and God. It builds resilience where today's children often have gaps.

Even adults struggle without that depth. Nicodemus, trained his whole life in Scripture, couldn't grasp the idea of spiritual rebirth. He had to sneak out in the middle of the night, embarrassed and confused, just to ask Jesus what He meant by being born again. Nicodemus wondered if he needed to return to his mother's womb and be re-delivered through the physical birth canal in order to acquire the spiritual birth Jesus spoke of. Nicodemus had knowledge and nothing more. If grown men can miss the deeper things of God with years of religious training, what happens to children?

How silly, especially coming from a well-known scholar like Nicodemus. This is what our children are getting, low levels of truth that do not hold them when deeper questions rise, anxiety builds, and puberty hits. God wants us to stop giving these kids milk because they have teeth. The world has exposed them to above average levels of materials and they need enough spiritual truths to be able to combat them.

What we all fail to understand is that when Jesus taught, he never taught on basic knowledge level, but He taught on a higher level that cultivated spiritual growth and development like we saw with the kids at the university in my dream.

This is why so many kids seem lost. Not because they're weak, but because we've given them nothing to stand on. No depth. No formation. No spiritual grounding that can hold them steady when life hits. Our kids must be trained in taking ownership of their faith through the freedom to ask questions, skill in finding answers, and reflections that deepen their belief.

Many adults are intimidated by the raw and unedited questions youth bring to the table because in all honesty, they fear not knowing God well enough to respond with the right answers. In an interview with Kara Powell, pastor, speaker, and writer, she states, "Our research has shown that struggle and doubt aren't toxic to faith. Silence and lack of trying are."

Willie's story shows us what's possible when a child is actually taught in a way that reaches their soul and not just their memory. It shows us the kind of faith that doesn't crumble. And honestly, that's the heartbeat of this chapter: helping the next generation grow roots deep enough to survive the storms heading their way.

Helping Youth Develop a Lasting Faith in Christ

If Willie's story teaches us anything, it's this: kids don't build a lasting faith by simply showing up at church or absorbing whatever their parents believe. Real faith doesn't stick because of association. It sticks because it's lived, explored, questioned, practiced, and repeated in the messy moments of everyday life.

This isn't a new idea. It's exactly how Paul trained Timothy. Paul didn't hand Timothy a curriculum packet and tell him to "go figure it out." Paul did not ask Timothy to recite Scripture he had memorized. He walked with him. He wrote to him. He corrected him, encouraged him, and reminded him not to shrink back just because he was young. More than anything, Paul let Timothy watch his life. He allowed Timothy to spend time with Him, see him cry, suffer, and overcome. Over time, Timothy learned how to lead and shepherd others because he'd first learned how to follow someone worth imitating.

Today's generation isn't asking for polished church routines; they're asking for something real. In the research from *You Lost Me*, young believers said one of the biggest factors that kept them anchored was simply experiencing conversation with God. Not a stiff, formal prayer life, but something alive. Something that felt like, "Talking to God and hearing from Him is actually part of who I am." When young people taste that kind of closeness with Christ, their identity starts to root itself in Him rather than drifting with every new pressure they face.

This desire for depth isn't new either. The Bereans in Acts 17:11 modeled it beautifully. They didn't just accept the message of Christ; they wanted to understand it. They examined, questioned, compared, studied, doubted it until they believed it, and lived out what they believed. Their faith wasn't second-hand. It became their own.

Somewhere along the way, youth ministry drifted from this. We filled schedules with programs, routines, and tidy lessons, but we left very little space for real encounters with God's Word. Think about Jesus' ministry: it happened in living rooms, on dirt roads, at dinner tables, in boats, and in raw moments of community. He taught while walking. He corrected in arguments. He restored people mid-meal. Everything was apprenticeship. Everything was life-on-life formation.

Compare that to many youth ministries today, which are often polished but hollow. Lots of structure, not much substance. Maybe that's why so many Generation Alpha kids feel connected to their online communities but disconnected from their faith communities. They're starving for relationship and depth, and they'll take it wherever they can find it.

George Barna nails the problem:

> "Another problem with the specialization of children's ministry is that we have created a faith that is simplified. It's a faith that kids grow out of instead of a robust faith that they grow into. Because of the desire to make things understandable, relatable, and relevant to kids, we have removed mystery. We've removed the paradox. When they bump up against something difficult, the simple Jesus they learned about when they were five can no longer help them in the complex world of their 20s, and so we inoculate them from the gospel."[8]

[8] George Barna, *Children's Ministry in a New Reality* (research report), 2023, emphasizing the risk of oversimplifying the gospel in ministry to kids and reducing their ability to grow into a robust faith.

We're seeing the impact of Barna's observation every day. Kids grow up knowing the Bible stories but not how to engage a God they can't see. They know church routines but not how to wrestle with doubts. They can retell David and Goliath but collapse under the weight of their own battles. It's not that they don't want faith. They just haven't been shown how to make it their own.

Scripture gives us a better model: apprenticeship. Jesus Himself lived it. He learned under His stepfather Joseph as a carpenter. He learned under God His Father, and He learned under the spiritual leaders of His day. Then He turned around and trained His disciples the same way. Not through lectures or sanitized lessons, but through relationship, repetition, correction, practice, and shared life.

If we want a generation with a faith that outlasts anxiety, pressure, confusion, and culture we have to return to the pattern and practices interwoven in Jesus' life story.

"You are in error because you do not know the Scriptures or the power of God."
(Matthew 22:29)

My Dream...

Kids Crave Seeing into the Windows of Heaven

A simple, yet symbolic dream, this showed how deep the spiritual hunger of our kids really runs.

I was standing outside a large, quiet home, watching a young child walk toward one of its tall windows. What I noticed first were his blue high-top sneakers with bright white laces. There was something kind of innocent and determined about the way he moved.

He walked with purpose, like he already knew the house held something important. When he reached the window, he stretched up on the tiptoe of his blue sneakers, lifting himself as high as he could. He raised his hands to the glass, trying to peek inside, hoping to catch even a small glimpse of what was happening in there.

Everything about him showed this mix of curiosity and longing, like he believed something good was waiting on the other side.

Chapter 4

The Questions They Search at 2:00 a.m.

Rodney was one of the most jubilant kids you would ever meet. Rising on Sunday morning to go to church with his family was one of his greatest joys. There was nothing greater than looking forward to the Christian camp during the summer. As Rodney grew into puberty and began facing inner battles, he struggled to find joy in going to church, or even summer camp. It was no longer a place that answered his increasingly complicated questions. Instead, he turned to the internet, where answers were always at his fingertips and he did not even need to ask his parents. In fact, he began arriving at church with what he believed were solid rebuttals to the biblical truths he heard from the pulpit, yet no one was engaging him deeply enough to challenge or guide him through them.

Although he challenged the structure in my classroom, another boy, JaQuan, was a student I felt honored to have in my class. He always surprised me with the most profound questions, both academic and personal. "Why we gotta do all this reading? Where do humans come from? And what is the reason why humans exist?" One day, JaQuan, tried to express in his eight-year-old vocabulary what he was facing. He said he had a good weekend and felt good on the outside, but on the inside, he had a problem. He shared how he'd stay up late at night watching videos till midnight. He expressed how He kept hearing voices that told him to kill himself and his classmates.

Grieved in the very crevices of my heart, I longed to take JaQuan and help him out in his struggles. How I longed to take the technology away from him and replace it with a modeled life that reflected who God was. How I craved the chance to speak God's Word over him and fervently and effectually pray against the voices he heard in his head that many youths committing crimes like these hear far before they act out on them.

Both Rodney and JaQuan ached for a depth that would counter their battles. They needed an antidote for the daily taunts against their souls.

I would go home and pray for JaQuan and Rodney privately, day after day, and I still do. For many children like JaQuan, church is not easily accessible, but social media always is. And even when church is available, their hardest questions are rarely answered in a way that exposes and uproots the darkness beneath them.

There's a hard truth we keep sidestepping. Most kids today aren't losing their faith because they're "rebellious" or "distracted." They're losing it because the version of Christianity they were handed was paper thin. Memorizing verses, sitting through Sunday talks, regurgitating what you learned from Scripture, and playing a couple of games made up what was commonly used for spiritual formation. It's the kind of faith a teenager can outgrow without even trying, especially when the noise of culture comes in like a tidal wave and fills every gap.

One of the first things any teacher learns is Bloom's Taxonomy. It's a ladder of learning, starting at the bottom with basic remembering, and climbing all the way up to analysis, evaluation, and finally something far deeper than information: self-actualization. That top level is where learning becomes part of who you are, not just something you can recite on command.

Here's an uncomfortable comparison. When it comes to culture, our youth climb straight to the top of that ladder. They apprentice themselves to the world without hesitation. They study their favorite influencers the same way past generations studied philosophers. They pick up the vocabulary, the symbols, the outlook, and they live it. Culture gives them a complete formation system. It teaches with application, clarity, boldness, repetition, rhythm, and immersion.

Yet when it comes to God, many of these same kids are still stuck on the bottom rung. They know a verse or two. They know enough to recognize a Bible story if you start the first line. The older and more sophisticated youth can even tell you if they side with Calvinist, Paul, or Arminianism. But few know how to ingest the very fiber of who Christ is into their lives.

They don't know how these truths fit deep down inside the real tensions of their lives. They have no spiritual language for identity, for mental pressure, for sexuality, for suffering, or for the mess that comes with growing up in this century. So, when those topics show up in full force, culture feels like the only source confident enough to answer them.

This is where the gap becomes dangerous.

Spiritually, many kids are underdeveloped, not because they lack interest, but because they lack apprenticeship. They don't have people around them modeling a mature, lived faith in close proximity. They're rarely invited to reflect, wrestle, question, meditate, apply, or practice. Without depth, they stay at the knowledge level, and knowledge alone cannot hold a young person steady in a world that synthesizes, analyzes, strategizes, and modifies.

They must not only be filled with the raw stories of the Bible, but they must be FILLED with what Jesus promised His disciples, and that is the precious Holy Spirit.

The Scriptures describe spiritual depth as moving from milk to meat. Milk is fine for the beginning, but it was never meant to be a lifelong diet. When youth stay on milk for too long, they end up with spiritual malnutrition. They know God in theory, but not in a way that can withstand pressure. And when pressure shows up, their faith bends, sometimes breaks, and often disappears altogether.

I can clearly remember the time God impressed upon me that this generation was to eat the meat of God's Word because of all the adult exposure they have encountered. Our children are now combatting what even adults struggle to overcome. The Word of God taught to our children can no longer remain at the surface level if our children are to survive the spiritual battles of our day.

Apprenticeship is the missing piece. When youth learn to walk with God through actual life, when they see faith modeled, practiced, questioned, and lived, they rise to the highest level of spiritual learning. They don't just know about God. They know Him for themselves in the context of their own story. Once that happens, culture no longer gets the final say. They do.

The Entrance of God's Word Brings Light

If there's one thing we've underestimated, it's how deeply kids can engage with Scripture when they're actually invited to. We put so much effort into helping them master sports, schoolwork, hobbies, and every skill under the sun, yet when it comes to the Bible, we barely scratch the surface. They're allowed to be curious everywhere except with the one thing that could shape their inner world.

Kids dive headfirst into whatever they love. They can memorize whole playlists, take apart video game lore, follow complicated plotlines, and explain scientific facts they learned from a five-minute video. But when it comes to God's Word, we rarely show them how to do more than listen politely. No one teaches them how to laugh at Scripture's surprises, feel the weight of its sadness, wrestle with its difficult passages, or sit quietly with a verse that hits too close. We forget that the Bible was always meant to be lived with, not glanced at.

When Scripture becomes clear, personal, and applicable something shifts inside a young person. The Bible calls it light, and that's exactly what it feels like. A steady glow. A clarity that doesn't disappear just because the world around them gets darker. Kids need permission to step into that kind of revelation, not as a chore, but as a discovery. Our kids are not too young to be filled with the revelation behind God's Word as well as be empowered by it.

I had the pleasure of traveling to see many of these things happen in real life at Veritas Christian Academy in Asheville, North Carolina during my research for my dissertation. One of the teachers there, Heidi Heiderich Dean, a youth Bible teacher, puts it better than anyone I've heard. She says the church has been so focused on teaching reverence and discipline that we kind of forgot about enjoyment—real enjoyment that makes students gasp, laugh, raise their eyebrows, ask questions, and light up when something finally clicks.

She talks about how her students react to Scripture the way kids react to a gripping novel or an intense movie scene. They respond with shock at the violence in Genesis, bashful grins at the story of Ruth and Boaz, and frustration over Israel's endless cycles in Judges.

She points out that these reactions aren't distractions—they're proof that the Word has come alive. Once that happens, kids remember it. They carry it with them. They live it and pass it on.

And think about it—what about kids diving into King David's messy choices? Or imagining John climbing that ladder into another dimension called heaven? That's the kind of raw, alive engagement that sticks with children.

Instead, many churches still use basic measurements for spiritual commitment: how many verses a child can memorize, how much they know and can regurgitate, copycat faiths of what they have heard discussed around them and whether they show up consistently. Those things aren't bad, but research keeps showing they don't predict lifelong faith. At times when they do, the child's faith is shallow and not one filled with depth. Kids need more than familiarity with the Bible. They need immersion. They need a faith that integrates with their current questions, battles, and doubts.

This is where apprenticeship fits perfectly with how the Generation Alpha's brains develop. Ages seven to twelve are a sweet spot. According to Swiss Psychologist Jean Piaget, this is when children shift from imaginative, anything-is-possible thinking to logic and organized reasoning. It's the perfect mix for spiritual growth. They can still believe without needing every detail explained, yet they're growing into the ability to analyze, question, and connect ideas. It's the perfect mix for spiritual growth. They can still believe without needing every detail explained, yet they're growing into the ability to analyze, question, and connect ideas.

At this age, they develop:

- Concrete logical thinking

They can understand cause and effect, follow sequences, and make sense of real-world examples. It's the ideal time to learn how Scripture plays out in everyday life.

- A dual mindset

They can believe in things that don't fully make sense while also beginning to think critically. That tension is the soil where real faith grows.

- Perspective-taking and empathy

They can consider multiple angles at once. They can look at a biblical passage and notice the history, the emotions, the tension, and the meaning beneath the surface.

This is why apprenticeship matters. Generation Alpha isn't too young, too distracted, or too impressionable. They're perfectly wired for depth. Perfectly wired for Scripture. Perfectly wired for encounters with God that stay with them.

We just have to stop handing them a dim, watered-down version of faith and instead show them how to step into the light.

Outward and Inner

We are all too familiar with the physical features of our kids, yet, we struggle to discern their inward development, what lens they perceive things through, and what battles they face.

Kids live in two different worlds. One is the version everyone sees: the smiles, the chatter, the school pictures, the cool apparel, the carefully curated hobbies, and the social media highlights. From the outside, they look full, confident, and put together. But beneath all of that energy and noise sits an inner world that's been running on empty for far too long. It's a place that aches for connection, emotional truth, and for someone to name the quiet struggles they don't have words for. It's the place where God has always been closest, yet the place most neglected in their upbringing.

Culture teaches kids how to present themselves, not how to know the Lord. They learn how to perform in sports, how to pose for photos, how to stay busy, and how to keep up with trends. They become experts at looking inflated on the outside while feeling deflated the moment they're alone. And if we could pull back the curtain on that inner world, we'd see the reality beneath the polish. We'd see fear. Questions. Confusion. Hunger. Desire. We'd see the God-shaped design inside them waiting for cultivation, and for someone to walk with them instead of around them. This is where spiritual apprenticeship comes in, where their inner world can be authentically seen and gracefully formed into the image of Christ.

The truth is uncomfortable: someone is shaping them, but it often isn't God. Research by the Barna Group found that adults raised in church held theological beliefs strikingly similar to those with no church background, and that fewer than one in ten churched teenagers possessed a biblical worldview. Their deepest formation comes from culture, not from apprenticeship or discipleship. Their worldview is delivered to them through a screen. Their imagination gets trained by whatever voices speak the loudest. And because their inner world sits untouched, it becomes easy for them to build identity on shifting ground.

This neglect shows through research highlighting what we already sense: our youth are struggling to understand who they are, to find mental wholeness, and to navigate sexuality without confusion or shame. These struggles aren't signs of rebellion; they're symptoms of spiritual starvation. Their souls are hungry, yet we keep feeding only the outward parts of their lives.

There are two worlds inside every child: the world we can see and the world we refuse to peer into. We spend endless energy developing the seen world. We make sure they're active, social, busy, and smiling. They sit in church with their bodies while their minds drift miles away. As long as they look fine, we treat them as if they are fine. Meanwhile, their unseen world stays untouched. No cultivation. No guidance. No space to breathe.

But if God formed both worlds, then both worlds need tending. This means more than moral reminders or busy programs. It means biblically rooted practices that speak directly to the soul and spirit, practices that awaken depth, identity, and purpose. Later in this book, I'll share the tools God has laid on my heart for this deeper work, but first we need to understand the other levels of this battleground.

Because I've lived in both spaces, from inner-city classrooms to church settings, the contrast is jarring. Kids as young as eight discuss culture with a level of blunt clarity that would shock most adults. Yet the topics that dominate their conversations barely get whispered in Christian spaces. The pulpit tiptoes around what culture shouts. The silence leaves our youth starving for guidance.

So, before we can rebuild anything, we need to name the places where the hunger is greatest.

There are three words the culture pronounces boldly while the church whispers them faintly: identity, mental wellness, and sexuality.

Engaging Youth in Identity, Mental Wellness, and Sexuality

From the moment babies are born, identity begins to be shaped: names, footprints, who they belong to, the family they're born into, and the uniformity of last names. But as kids grow, layers like friends, beliefs, and traditions add to that foundation. For Generation Alpha, there's more at play: social media, school pressures, technology, and new autonomy all shape identity in ways that didn't exist before.

Mental wellness is another huge piece of the puzzle. Loneliness, bullying, and online pressure ... these aren't small bumps on the road. They're shaping the mental and emotional landscape of youth. Studies show churchgoing teens often believe spiritual growth is something they do alone rather than in community. Yet God's design is for connection, guidance, and community. The peace Christ offers isn't just a feel-good idea, it's a real inheritance meant to counter anxiety, fear, and confusion.

Sexuality, identity, and mental wellness are deeply interconnected. And yet, so often, youth ministry and Bible instruction treat these areas lightly—through memorization, routines, and fun activities—but rarely give kids the tools to own their faith, understand themselves, or navigate the complex pressures of life. This leaves youth vulnerable to culture, spiritually undernourished, and disconnected from Christ in ways they don't even fully realize.

Engaging in God's Word must go deeper than surface-level teaching. There must be a merging of where youth are and who God is. There must be a sense of youth being a partaker and stakeholder engaged in personal ownership. There must be a sense of immersion from the world and culture they live in to the world and culture God lives in.

Engaging with God should be a place where anxieties are released, identities are affirmed, and sexuality is understood in the context of God's love. The Word, carefully unpacked, scaffolded, and applied, brings light into their lives. Psalm 119:130 says, *"The unfolding of Your words gives light; it gives understanding to the simple."* That's exactly what youth need: light in the middle of confusion, clarity in the middle of questions, and a God who is real and near.

Jesus told the Pharisees that in Scripture, they thought they had eternal life (John 5:39). Yet they refused to go to Him for eternal life. Jesus saw their way of learning about Him as the lowest level of learning; they were just skimming through the surface with no root or depth. He had a better way for them to grow in spiritual depth. Jesus wanted them to know that Scripture had substance behind it that brought forth life-giving enlightenment, and they had not reached that level of learning and growth in their spiritual journey. God does not want this replicated in our youth. He hears their cry against the mundane, the boredom, and the lack of relevance from their lives to what is taught in church, and God wants this low level of instruction changed. This is truly how the entrance of what God means in Scripture brings forth light.

Youth today see a huge gap between church culture and the real world. Even well-meaning adults often struggle to engage meaningfully across differences, leaving kids feeling alienated from Christ's love. But there is hope. Spiritual apprenticeship, deep engagement with God's Word, and intentional mentoring can bridge that gap. Youth can encounter Christ in ways that are real, personal, and lasting. They can experience communion, transformation, and freedom that culture alone can never provide.

And this brings us to the heart of it... God sees it all. Every struggle, every tear, every question, every anxiety, every sexual battle, and every injustice. Our children want to know that they have a God who understands their frustrations and walks with them through suffering. One of the most powerful illustrations of this truth comes from a well-known anonymous Christian teaching illustration that has been widely shared in ministry settings. The story vividly captures humanity's longing to know whether God truly understands our pain and whether He is truly worthy to judge the human condition.

> "At the end of time, billions of people were scattered on a great plain before God's throne. Most shrank back from the brilliant light before them. But some groups near the front talked heatedly – not with cringing shame, but with belligerence.

"How can God judge us? How can he know about suffering?" snapped an older woman. She ripped open a sleeve to reveal a tattooed number from a Nazi concentration camp. *"We endured terror...beatings... torture...death!"*

In another group, a black man lowered his collar. *"What about this?"* he demanded, showing an ugly rope burn. *"Lynched...for no crime but being black!"*

In another crowd, a pregnant young girl with sullen eyes stepped forward. *"Why should I suffer?"* she murmured, *"He took advantage of me."*

Far out across the plain, there were many such groups. Each had a complaint against God for the evil and suffering He permitted in His world.

"How lucky God was," they seemed to say, "to live in heaven where all was sweetness and light, where there was no weeping or fear, no hunger or hatred." What did God know of all that humans had been forced to endure in this world? "God leads a pretty sheltered life", they said. "What right does He have to evaluate our lives?"

So, each of these groups sent forth its leader, chosen because he or she had suffered most. A Jew, a Black man, a person from Hiroshima, a horribly deformed arthritic, a child who was a victim of human trafficking, and several others. In the center of the plain, they consulted with each other.

At last, they were ready to present their case. It was rather clever.

Before God could be qualified to be their judge, He must endure what they had endured. They decided that God should be sentenced to live on earth as a human man! One by one, they proclaimed their conditions.

"Let him be born into a poor, conquered country and into a despised minority group...perhaps a Jew.

Let the legitimacy of his birth be doubted.

Let him lose a parent early in life.

Give him a work so difficult that even his family will think him out of his mind when he tries to do it.

Let his motives be misunderstood.

Let him experience extreme temptations and deprivation.

Let him be betrayed by his closest friends.

Let him face false charges, be tried by a prejudiced jury, and convicted by a cowardly judge.

Let him be tortured horribly."

"At the last, let him experience what it means to be so terribly alone. Then let him die painfully. Let him die so violently that there can be no doubt that he died. Let there be a great host of witnesses to verify his death."

As each leader announced his portion of the sentence, loud murmurs of approval went up from the throng of people assembled.

When the last had finished pronouncing sentence, there was a long silence. Slowly, smug smiles disappeared. No one uttered another word. No one moved...except for heads bowing in shame. For suddenly, all knew the staggering truth: **that God had already served His sentence.**[9]

[9] https://www.challies.com/quotes/the-long-silence/

Not only has God served His sentence (which He never deserved), but He's also served our sentence. Our sin does not have to separate us from the love of God. He sent His Son to redeem us from sin and to claim us as His spiritual bride.

God sees every youth. Every battle, every tear, and every question is known. Because Christ has already walked the path of suffering and redemption, every child, teen, and young adult can find refuge, hope, and light. They don't have to navigate culture, anxiety, or identity alone. Christ is their anchor, their teacher, their guide, and their storyteller, and the apprenticeship of a lifetime is waiting for them.

"Do not arouse or awaken love until it so desires."
(Song of Solomon 8:4)

My Dream...

Kids Reaching Heaven

I found myself in a foreign country. It felt like somewhere in Europe or the United Kingdom, full of old stone buildings, beautiful landscapes, and the kind of scenery that makes you slow down and pay attention. A group of young children was with me, and we wandered and played our way through this new place with the same carefree energy you'd see in The Sound of Music.

At one point, a tour guide joined us and began pointing out different areas, helping us understand where we were. Eventually we reached a high lookout above a wide body of water. As we stood there, the children and I began to worship God in song. Their voices grew stronger and stronger, rising from deep inside them, as if their singing stretched all the way toward heaven.

Something shifted in that moment. The atmosphere changed, almost like it thickened with God's presence. People nearby, both locals and tourists, stopped to watch. Some bowed their heads and joined in. Then something even more unexpected happened. Angels appeared and joined us in worship. The whole scene felt sacred and completely beyond anything earthly.

When I woke up, the dream stayed with me. It felt vivid and meaningful, especially the pure love the children poured out in worship and the way

God responded with His presence and His angels. Interpreting dreams has never been simple for me. Some take months or even years to understand. But this one felt clear.

The foreign country represented new spiritual territory, places where children can grow strong enough to face their battles. Worship in the dream pointed to the way faith brings us into unity with God. The tour guide reminded me of the Holy Spirit leading us into truth. And the angels showed the protection and nearness God gives to those who draw close to Him. If the culture can make provisions for young children to cultivate sexuality before it is time, why can't godly parents cultivate a close opportunity through worship that will attach youth to Christ for a lifetime.

Our children need to know they are welcome in God's presence. They need to know the wonder of encountering Him for themselves. When we, as parents and leaders, aren't intentional about helping them experience God, that baton of faith can easily slip from their hands. But the dream reminded me of this: our kids are not alone. The first level of intimacy that should awaken their hearts should take place with Christ. When that takes place, no other level of intimacy will be able to compare with the touch they felt in the presence of a lavishly loving God. God and his heavenly hosts are with them for their whole journey as they learn to worship and walk with Him.

Chapter 5

A Sexual Culture that Engages Kids

Teikeya was in my third-grade class when I noticed she was talking to her peers about inappropriate content. I took her to a quiet space and asked where she was learning this type of information.

She quietly told me that her friend, Sunny, had been talking about a video she saw online with a boy and girl kissing and doing "nasty stuff." Kids shouldn't have to sort through things like that, but here we are.

I pulled Sunny into the hallway and asked her about it. She said the video popped up while she was playing a game, and even though she wanted to stop watching, she froze and didn't know what to do. When I asked if she told her parents, she said her mom had caught her and talked to her, but the images were still stuck in her mind. She honestly didn't know how to get them out. I shared the situation with her parents and the school counselor. Moments like this remind you how much kids really carry without anyone noticing.

Corey was another student in my class. One day he told me that his mom would be taking him to the doctor to keep his voice and body from changing into that of a man.

It was one of those moments where you realize how early these conversations are happening now. I kindly listened, then stopped myself from going further since after all, I was in a public-school setting.

Behind the curtains of Sunny's and Corey's physical lives and activities lie their souls waiting to be formed into the spirit that God intended them to be.

What weighs on me are the long-term effects for kids who make big, permanent changes before they're old enough to fully understand themselves. Some later realize they feel differently, but the physical changes can't simply be reversed. All of this is happening in a generation already battling unprecedented mental-health challenges. Suicide is now the second leading cause of death for young people ages 10–24, according to the National Alliance on Mental Illness[10].

Jesus understood the sexually broken in a way that was both honest and deeply compassionate. He didn't shame them. He didn't push them away. Instead, He used moments of worship and connection to draw them back to Himself. Think of the woman at the well, whose long search for acceptance finally met its match in Jesus offering her living water so she would never thirst again. Or Mary, sitting at His feet for hours, listening, learning, soaking in every word. Or the woman who poured out her past and her pain as she washed His feet with her hair. Even the woman caught in adultery freed from the condemnation of her community through Jesus. Jesus is fully aware of the challenges by youth and sexuality. Scripture is full of these moments where worship becomes a bridge for the hurting.

[10] National Alliance on Mental Illness (NAMI): Suicide is the second leading cause of death among people ages 10–14 and 15–24 in the U.S.

Worship is any act that points youth back to their heavenly Father. Worship is an abandonment of self for the purpose of giving God the best part of what we believe.

Worship still plays that role today, especially for our kids. It gives them a way to connect with a God they can't physically see, and it speaks to places in their hearts that everyday conversations can't always reach. This kind of grounding is needed more than ever.

The reality of our culture is how early kids are being pulled into sexual messaging. Before they even understand the meaning of what they're seeing, they're being flooded with images, terms, symbols, colors, and identity cues from social media and beyond. They're being shaped long before they realize it.

One of the hardest battles young people face today, in a way past generations didn't, is growing up in a culture that pushes sexual content at them from every direction. It shows up in their music, their shows, their social feeds, even in the ways their peers talk. It's a lot for a young mind to carry, especially when they're still trying to figure out who they are. Scripture teaches that we are not to awaken love until the proper time (Song of Solomon 8:4), suggesting that sexuality and romantic emotions are meant to develop in healthy, appropriate stages rather than being rushed.

Unlike a culture that often exposes children to sexual themes before they are emotionally or spiritually ready, worship offers a pure and healthy way for children to express love for God. Through worship, children can express heartfelt devotion through music, dance, art, and prayer. These forms of expression are not only healthy for their emotional and spiritual development but also help create a deeper connection with God that anchors their faith and shapes their spiritual identity.

In turn, our youth receive something greater and more sacred. They receive God's love for them. Worship becomes a kind of refuge for them. It's like a steady, life-giving stream that reaches places inside them that nothing else can touch. When kids enter worship, they're not just singing or expressing themselves to God. They're stepping into a place where they can breathe again, where their hearts feel seen, and where God's presence meets them right in the middle of everything they're dealing with. For a young person being hit with constant sexual messages and pressures, that kind of spiritual grounding is more than comforting. It's necessary.

Most of our children know the story of David and Goliath. They know the victory, the bravery, and the triumph. Yet we avoid the painful story of David's affair with Bathsheba and everything that happened as a result. And maybe that gap matters more than we realize.

It might even explain why so many of our kids end up walking through the same struggles as kids who never grew up with faith at all. Statistics show that sexual activity among young teens is increasing. According to the Centers for Disease Control (CDC), almost one in ten teenagers had sexual intercourse before turning thirteen, and the trend is climbing. Pornography makes the situation even heavier, feeding a level of sexualization that kids simply aren't equipped to process.

Children's ministry leaders feel the weight of this. Thirty-seven percent say they're worried about not discipling kids well when it comes to these hard topics. Many leaders admit they're unsure how to talk about sexual pressures in a healthy, age-appropriate way. And on top of that, some leaders quietly struggle with porn and other sexual battles themselves, which only makes the challenge feel more complicated.

Despite all this, most churches don't have any structured program or ministry to help kids, families, or leaders face these realities. The need is real, and the gap is wide. Our children are hurting, and God has made space for their healing. It's up to us to step into that space with them.

These days, confusion about human sexuality has really shaken the way traditional Christian values are understood, and that pressure lands on young believers in a huge way. Seven out of ten teens now say it's okay to feel like a different gender than the one they were born with, and almost half think it's fine for someone to physically change their body to match that feeling.

From a biblical counseling perspective, Christian author and pastor, Paul David Tripp, emphasizes that human sexuality is not merely about physical desire or emotion but flows from the deeper condition of the heart and one's relationship with God. In his book *Sex in a Broken World: How Christ Redeems What Sin Distorts*, Tripp challenges believers to see sexuality through the lens of the gospel — not as a standalone urge or instinct, but as something defined within covenant and shaped by God's design for human flourishing.

He explains that:

> "You will suffer the reality that right here, right now, sex doesn't function the way that God intended … this broken world is waiting for redemption … Sex confronts me with my inability. As I examine myself in light of God's standard of absolute purity, I fall down with Paul and say, 'I know that nothing good lives in me, that is, in my sinful nature.' … Sex reveals my need of grace."[11]

This framing underscores that authentic Christian sexuality is about the covenantal union of husband and wife as a sign of God's faithful

[11] Paul David Tripp, *Sex in a Broken World: How Christ Redeems What Sin Distorts* (Wheaton, IL: Crossway, 2018), 16–23.

relationship with His people and that any expression of sexuality apart from that covenant reflects deeper heart issues that point back to identity, worship, and grace — not merely the physical act itself.

When sexuality gets twisted, through casual hookups, recreational encounters, abuse, gender confusion, underage experimentation, or addiction, it's no longer what it was designed to be. And that distortion affects our kids deeply. Here's a snapshot of where today's youth are in terms of sexual wholeness and the influences shaping their understanding.

In the Area of Sexuality

- The CDC reports that almost one out of every ten teenagers had sexual intercourse prior to his or her thirteenth birthday and that number is steadily rising.
- A 2024 study found a significant decrease in youth identifying as heterosexual, from 84.5 percent to 74. percent, from 2019 to 2021. (Pew Research)
- Seven out of ten youth say it is acceptable to be born one gender and feel like another, while two out of five contend it is okay for someone to change their body to another gender.
- A recent national survey of young adults ages twenty-five to thirty reports more than a quarter of them first viewed pornography before puberty.
- A 2014 brain imaging study published in *JAMA Psychiatry* found that frequent pornography use was linked to changes in parts of the brain connected to reward and motivation. The researchers observed a pattern called habituation, which means that over time, repeated exposure can make the same material feel less stimulating. As a result, some individuals may begin seeking more novel or intense content to experience the same level of excitement.

Much of God's standards or even the repercussions of sin are not fully discussed with our youth. The culture is louder than the spiritual leaders on the topic of sexuality, especially when it comes to our youth.

My experience in the classroom is that children today are not familiar with the biblical concept of the rainbow. Instead, they automatically tie it in with transgenderism and the LGBTQ community. We can look past the flood, when God gave a rainbow to His people as a sign of His covenant. He directed them to make it a practice of looking at the rainbow as a reminder of not only the covenant He made with them but the covenant He had for youth of the following generations. Our lack of attention to the directives God gave behind the rainbow demonstrates the detrimental impact that the lack of practices and symbols can have on youth. A whole generation has shifted views on the original intent behind the rainbow because the practice of looking at God's creation as a means for it to point back to Him has become inactive.

In Genesis 19 God said, "This is the sign of the covenant I am making between me and you and every living creature with you, a covenant for all generations to come: I have set my rainbow in the clouds, and it will be the sign of the covenant between me and the earth."

While the rainbow that now waves over our culture is designed slightly differently, few are aware of the differences and conclude that the rainbow stands as a symbol of sexual identity.

Long before our culture turned the rainbow into a symbol of sexual identity, God established it as a sign we could point our youth to as a promise He made between Himself and them. It was a practice of observation meant to be passed down through generations.

The Power of Practice in Worship

Our kids are being shaped every day, whether we realize it or not. What they watch, scroll through, listen to, and talk about is forming their understanding of love, identity, and sexuality. Those messages are repeated constantly, and repetition shapes desire. If the only repeated formation they receive comes from culture, we should not be surprised when culture defines their values.

That is why worship cannot be reduced to a weekly event. Worship is not just singing songs on Sunday. It is the steady habit of turning attention back to God. When children learn to pause, pray honestly, reflect on Scripture, notice beauty in creation, or express their faith through music or art, they are practicing something deeper than performance. They are learning how to relate to God in real time.

Practices matter because information alone does not shape the heart. A child can memorize verses and still feel lost when facing anxiety, temptation, or confusion about identity. Faith becomes resilient when it is practiced, not just explained. Just as repetition trains desire in a sexualized culture, repetition in worship trains the heart to seek God.

We sometimes make this harder than it needs to be. Bible characters are often presented as spiritual superheroes, which can make kids quietly assume that faith is for people who have it all together. But the people in Scripture struggled. They doubted, failed, wrestled, and questioned. When we allow children to see that reality, faith becomes something they can step into, not something they feel excluded from.

What young people need are tools they can actually use. They need to know how to pray when they feel overwhelmed, how to confess when they have given in to temptation, how to sit with God when they are confused about their feelings, and how to worship even when their emotions are complicated. These habits do not eliminate struggle, but they teach children that their struggles belong in God's presence, not outside of it.

Over time, those repeated practices anchor identity. Instead of being defined by impulse, comparison, or cultural pressure, they begin to understand themselves as known and loved by God. That kind of formation does not happen accidentally. It grows through consistent, honest engagement with Him.

Sexual Shame

Sexual shame began in the garden when Adam and Eve's eyes were opened after disobeying God's command. Following this disobedience was the embarrassment that both Adam and Eve felt, to the point that they covered their bodies with leaves. Today, this shame is starting with the youngest generation that exists. The antidote to the sexual shame is obedience to God's Word, which is the ultimate act of worship. Teaching kids in detail what true worship looks like can save a whole generation from the repercussions of sexual shame in their spiritual journey.

> *"But our citizenship is in heaven. And we eagerly await a Savior from there, the Lord Jesus Christ, who, by the power that enables him to bring everything under his control, will transform our lowly bodies so that they will be like his glorious body."*
> *(Philippians 3:20-21)*

My Dream...

From Death to Life

I was in the outdoor plains of a foreign country; I stood above a deep ground prepared for burial. Somehow, I began to find my way down this burial ground, walking down into it. Finally, I laid down as if I was going to sleep. A little while later, I arose, and it seemed like angelic beings were helping me up. One cupped my head in their hand. Gradually, I sat up and walked out of that grave. Jesus stood at the opposite end from which I entered the grave to greet me. As I stood before Him, I realized my apparel was different. I had walked in with some jeans and a top and rose with a white robe. I looked as if I was from a different culture, and we spoke a language that was not common to me. He greeted me with His right hand, and I now belonged to Him.

Chapter 6

Raising Royalty in a Kingless Age

But you are a chosen people, a royal priesthood, a holy nation, God's special possession, that you may declare the praises of him who called you out of darkness into his wonderful light. (1 Peter 2:9)

As our children get to know God as their personal identity, it will become very important for them to shift their mindset from a citizen of this Earth to one that fits into the citizenship of Christ. Not being anchored in this spiritual concept can keep them hostage in many ways that are against the ways of God. The Scripture found in Romans 12:2 states it so clearly, "Do not conform to the pattern of this world, but be transformed by the renewing of your mind. Then you will be able to test and approve what God's will is—his good, pleasing and perfect will."

This should not be a one-and-done teaching for our youth but one that is constantly layered with conversations, models, stories, and practices. This is not an admonishment to be weird and awkward, but an admonishment to be whatever Christ has called them to be. As they change their minds in not conforming to the culture around them, they will begin to perceive what it is that God is calling them to be and to do in His name.

Our children must understand this concept before they can move further in their faith. Consider a man of a foreign country and one that worshiped idols living a life contrary to God. Abraham had to leave his country and learn of the new place God had for Him. It was all new, but it was possible, and little by little, not only did Abraham get to know of His new Father which was God, but He, too, duplicated His father's identity and became the Father of many sons. Our children are called to the same pathway.

"These are a shadow of the things that were to come; the reality, however, is found in Christ." (Colossians 2:17). "They serve at a sanctuary that is a copy and shadow of what is in heaven." (Hebrews 8:5).

Have you ever seen a child side by side with his father? The resemblance rings true—the child echoes so many of their father's features: they may have the same smile, the same nose, the same hair, and all the things that say, "This is their child." Yet we know the child is not the father. The child carries some of the father's blueprint; likewise, in many ways, our children can grow to spiritually embody God's blueprint. This can often be considered resemblance, or for our purpose, shadows.

In the Bible, "shadows" represent incomplete realities, foreshadowing greater spiritual truths in Christ. As image bearers, children must understand these shadows because they point to the why's behind who they are and who God is. Without a solid understanding of the shadows in Scripture that point to God, our kids will struggle to establish a faith that can stand against the culture they face every day.

Shadows liken God as the groom and the church as the bride, God as our Father, and God's presence as our peace. These are all crucial in building foundations of truth—foundations that can cause a child's faith to last a lifetime.

If we teach our kids that God is the original blueprint, they will better understand the imprints in their lives that exist to glorify Him. Our youth must come to understand that God is the complete supremacy when it comes to authority, sexuality, mental rest, and identity.

One of the most profound things God showed me as I searched to understand why Generation Alpha struggles so much with their spirituality is found in Matthew 22:29: "We do greatly err in not knowing the Scriptures." Not allowing our kids to feed on God's Word and the revelations behind it is one of the key reasons our children are falling astray.

It happened to the children in the book of Judges, where it states there was a generation that did not know the Lord (Judges 2:10). This generation had no clue of their history, what their forefathers had experienced with God, or what it meant to have an identity connected to Him. This lack of understanding impacted how they lived, how they expressed their sexuality, and how they faced darkness, the absence of God, and even anxiety. The book of Judges shows us what life looked like without a solid understanding of God in one's life.

Generation Alpha in God's Government

Understanding the difference between a kingdom mindset and a democratic mindset is essential when thinking about Generation Alpha and their spiritual formation. Because of where many of the children are born and raised, it can be difficult for them to grasp what God's government truly represents. Take those born in the United States, for example—they have a socially progressive mindset, which can work to their advantage. Yet when it comes to God's kingdom, they may feel confused.

Generation Alpha is very clear about their freedom of expression, their rights, their authority, and their sense of diversity and fairness. But if they are not taught that God existed before anything or anyone else and that He has complete authority over all, it can become a problem when they read about His standards and ways in many vernaculars. Because as 1 Peter states, "*But ye are a chosen generation, a royal priesthood, a holy nation, a peculiar people; that ye should shew forth the praises of him who hath called you out of darkness into his marvelous light*" (*1 Peter 2:9*). God's standards are often contrary to the standards in modern-day cultures. This must be explicitly explained so that children are clear about the standards governing their citizenship in Christ.

More than just knowing that Christ was crucified for their sins, they must also understand that He did not abandon them and leave them alone.

The Comforter Follows the Crucifixion

Kids raised in the church are well-versed about Jesus dying on the cross for their sins, yet they know very little about the power that raised Christ from the dead and the Comforter He left for His people following the Ascension. In times where youth are battling loneliness, suicide, and leaving the Christian faith, our youth must be layered with the power that is found in Christ and the presence of His power at times when they face challenges. The Comforter, otherwise known as the Holy Spirit, is an essential part of the godly journey for youth. They can be assured that God's presence always accompanies them even in times of danger. Young Willie from our previous chapters, was aware of the Holy Spirit and redeemed the prize of safety even in the attempt of a kidnapper's attempt to harm him. Our kids can rely on the Holy Spirit to deepen their faith. The Holy Spirit is there to lead our children into all truths.

God's Government

Generation Alpha must know that in God's government, there is a king, and God is that king. As part of His government, we are His kingdom. Jesus left a description of how His kingdom would be empowered, and our children must become familiar with this depiction of the people who come to know Him as Lord. Matthew 5:3-12 gives us the words of Jesus from The Sermon on the Mount, which describes virtues God values. They are as follows:

He said:

3 *"Blessed are the poor in spirit,*
for theirs is the kingdom of heaven.
4 *Blessed are those who mourn,*
for they will be comforted.
5 *Blessed are the meek,*
for they will inherit the earth.
6 *Blessed are those who hunger and thirst for righteousness,*
for they will be filled.
7 *Blessed are the merciful,*
for they will be shown mercy.
8 *Blessed are the pure in heart,*
for they will see God.
9 *Blessed are the peacemakers,*
for they will be called children of God.
10 *Blessed are those who are persecuted because of righteousness,*
for theirs is the kingdom of heaven.

11 *"Blessed are you when people insult you, persecute you and falsely say all kinds of evil against you because of me.*

12 *Rejoice and be glad, because great is your reward in heaven, for in the same way they persecuted the prophets who were before you.*

Many of these depictions are far from what Generation Alpha sees as part of their governing stance. What they may see as normal, such as having their opinions count, making decisions for themselves, and expecting their voices to matter, can actually make it tricky for them to understand God's kingdom. They're used to a more collaborative, "everyone gets a say" kind of world. But God's kingdom works differently. It's not about votes or personal preference, rather it's about trusting a King whose ways are perfect and whose authority doesn't change. For kids growing up in this fast, digital, instant-feedback culture, slowing down to submit to God's ways can feel really hard, even frustrating. That's why helping them see the difference between the way the world works and God's kingdom is so important for shaping their identity and faith.

Sexuality and Gender Confusion

When it comes to gender roles and sexuality, the world is confusing—even for adults—so how can we expect kids to have it all figured out? A lot of the trouble starts when we don't explain Scripture clearly to them. We give them shallow answers that barely touch the core of who they are. While culture is shouting its messages through social media, TV, and everywhere else, the kids aren't always hearing the truth from the people who love them most.

Ephesians 5:31 says, "Therefore a man shall leave his father and mother and hold fast to his wife, and the two shall become one flesh.' This mystery is profound, and I am saying that it refers to Christ and the church." This Scripture is often used to declare the roles of marriage, yet, there is so much more to it. It is not so much about the roles of a husband and a wife, but more of a shadow that points to God. Jesus came to Earth, leaving His Father in heaven. He came as a provider, a Savior, one that would cleave to us as His bride. We, as the bride, are receptors of God's sacrifice, and these roles can never be reversed. God provides for us and we receive. These are the shadows that point to Christ through our genders as we are appointed image bearers. The role of God in our lives and our roles as His provision for us can never be reversed, neither can they be modified and man-made.

Many in Generation Alpha do not have solid foundations as their anchor. Therefore, it is easy for them to accept the concept that gender roles are optional and they have the authority to switch, flip, and swipe what gender they want to be. When Scriptures like Ephesians are scaffolded, demonstrating that we are image bearers of a greater blueprint, kids can more easily become anchored in their understanding of gender roles and not be swayed by what culture defines as gender roles. It is not God who points to marriage as a standard, but marriage that points to God's relationship with the church.

Subsequently, in Matthew 22:30, it says, *"At the resurrection people will neither marry nor be given in marriage; they will be like the angels in heaven."* This shows that the true blueprint and significance of marriage is revealed through our relationship with God. Marriage, as we know it on Earth, won't exist in eternity. This is because in God, the greatest love of all would have been consummated when we go to live with Him forever. Marriage again, is just a shadow to glorify God. Our kids need to grasp this, so they aren't confused about gender roles in earthly relationships.

Grounding youth in these foundational truths means teaching them from books of the Bible that clearly show God's plan and authority. Some of these key books include Genesis, Deuteronomy, and the Gospels, among others. These stories help kids understand God's original blueprint and His design for sexuality.

Identity

In 1 Corinthians 4:15, Paul tells the Corinthian church, "Even if you had ten thousand guardians in Christ, you do not have many fathers, for in Christ Jesus I became your father through the gospel."

Our kids have plenty of teachers—adults who guide them, experiences that shape them, and technology that informs them—but often, the nurturing love, the authority, and the patient time investment of a true father figure is missing. This gap has fueled an identity crisis in our youth. They can easily latch onto anything that gives them a sense of belonging.

One helpful way to understand spiritual identity is by considering the role of DNA. A child is recognized as belonging to their parents because of a shared biological inheritance. In the same way, our youth carry a spiritual inheritance. Yet many have not been given the depth, language, or formation needed to fully recognize God as their Father.

The following reflection draws from a theological framework articulated by Author and Bible Teacher Portia Collins, re-examined here in the context of spiritual formation and identity.

[12]Scripture identifies Abraham as the father of faith, a man whose belief in God's promise was counted to him as righteousness (Genesis 15:6). Beyond his role in history, Abraham's life prophetically points forward to the coming of the Messiah in meaningful and layered ways.

In Genesis 12:1, God calls Abraham to leave what is familiar—his land, his people, his security—and journey toward an unknown place. This call requires radical trust. In response to Abraham's obedience, God promises to form from him a great nation, to bless him, and to make his name significant so that he might become a blessing to others (Genesis 12:2). Abraham's willingness to submit to God's direction reflects the posture later embodied by Jesus Christ. Just as Abraham obeyed without knowing the full outcome, Christ submitted fully to the will of the Father, even when obedience led Him to the cross (Philippians 2:8). Jesus Himself affirms this posture when He explains that the Son of Man

[12] Portia Collins, *"How Old Testament Typology Reveals Shadows of Salvation,"* https://www.logos.com/grow/nook-typology-old-testament/.

came not to be served, but to serve, and to give His life as a ransom for many (Matthew 20:28).

Abraham's identity as a father further anticipates the relationship between God the Father and Jesus Christ. In Genesis 22, God tests Abraham by asking him to offer his son, Isaac, as a sacrifice. Although Isaac was not Abraham's only child, he was the son of promise—the one through whom God declared that Abraham's legacy and nation would come (Genesis 17:19–21). Abraham's willingness to surrender Isaac reveals a profound trust in God and prefigures the Father's own willingness to offer His Son for the redemption of humanity.

Both Isaac and Jesus are described in Scripture as beloved sons, and in both accounts, the offering is made in obedience to God's will. At the critical moment, God intervenes and spares Isaac, providing a ram as a substitute sacrifice (Genesis 22:11–13). This act of substitution points forward to the ultimate substitutionary sacrifice of Jesus Christ, through whom believers receive reconciliation with God (1 Peter 3:18).

Identity in Christ is something our children can truly carry as image bearers of God. For that to happen, they need to understand the story of identity that begins with Adam, continues through Abraham, and is ultimately fulfilled in Christ. They need to be immersed in the revelation of who God is and what His purpose has always been for humanity.

These are the kinds of stories that ground young people in God's blueprint for identity.

Mental Wellness

Another powerful shadow in Scripture is peace. As image bearers, our children actually have an inheritance of peace, yet so many of them have never learned how to access it. Throughout my years of teaching, I have watched countless children wrestle with anxiety, depression, ADHD, and deep inner unrest.

Our children need to know that mental turmoil did not begin with them. Peace was first lost in the Garden of Eden. Today's Generation Alpha carries some of the highest levels of anxiety and emotional overload, yet without understanding the origin of unrest through the stories of Adam and Eve, the Israelites in Egypt, Jesus' anguish in the Garden of Gethsemane, and finally the victory won at the cross, they cannot fully grasp the peace that is now available to them in Christ.

As image bearers, they must come to understand that God is not distant from their anxiety. He has always been aware of human suffering and has always been moving toward redemption. They need to see the agony in Adam and Eve's story and then follow the thread of how God steps in to restore. Mental distress did not start with this generation, and it was ultimately defeated at the cross. Our children are longing to know that this victory is not just historical but personal, and that the peace of God can become real in their own lives.

Generation Alpha also needs to be rooted in the story of how the Israelites cried out in Egypt and how God rescued them, not only by freeing them from slavery but by giving them the gift of rest. Through the Sabbath, their identity shifted. They were no longer defined as brick makers or valued for what they produced. They were given a new identity as a people who were loved, received, and cared for by God, apart from what they could accomplish.

This is the kind of rest our children desperately need today. They need to understand that their identity is not built on performance, achievement, or productivity, but on who God is and who He has created them to be in Him.

Closing Reflections –The Problem

In this section, we have been sitting with the layers of problems facing this young generation. We have listened to the questions rising in classrooms, the confusion around identity, the silent battles with anxiety and mental unrest, the pressure surrounding sexuality, and the deep hunger for belonging and truth. We have seen children like Jared, Rodney, and JaQuan searching for something solid to stand on, something real enough to hold the weight of their fears, doubts, and longings.

Through the prophetic dreams, we viewed the spiritual reality behind these struggles. Again and again, the message was clear: our children are not just facing social or emotional challenges, they are in a spiritual battle for identity, safety, truth, and belonging, and only Jesus has the authority to rescue them.

We explored how Generation Alpha is growing up in a world that speaks loudly but anchors them poorly, offering information without any wisdom, freedom without any direction, and identity without any roots. We also looked at how Scripture reveals deeper patterns, shadows, and blueprints that point to who God is and who our children are meant to be in Him. We traced how confusion about authority, peace, gender, and belonging is not new, but how the lack of grounding in God's story leaves this generation especially vulnerable.

It's important to know that this section has not been about blaming culture or shaming children; it has been about listening, slowing down enough to hear the cry beneath the behavior, recognizing that beneath the noise, the screens, the opinions, and the struggles, there is a generation quietly asking, "Who am I? Am I safe? Do I belong? Is God real, and does He hear me?"

And now, having named the problem, we are ready to turn toward "The Answer."

"These commandments that I give you today are to be on your hearts. Impress them on your children. Talk about them when you sit at home and when you walk along the road, when you lie down and when you get up."
Deuteronomy 6:6-7

PART II

THE ANSWER

Section Preview

Every cry of Generation Alpha ultimately leads to one place: Jesus. But for our children to truly know Him as their answer, they must first understand who He is, what He faced, and how He learned to walk in identity, obedience, and intimacy with the Father.

In this section, we slow down and look at Jesus not just as the Savior, but as a child, a student, a Son, and finally a Savior.

We talk about His early years, His growth, and the way He was formed spiritually and emotionally. These are parts of His story that often get skipped, yet they help our kids realize, "He understands what I'm going through."

We'll also walk through real people in the Bible who faced fear, temptation, identity struggles, and inner battles—very much like what our youth face today—and how Jesus became their answer in the middle of it all.

And finally, we'll look at the simple but powerful practices Jesus lived by to stay connected to His Father. Not religious routines, but real-life rhythms that can fit into everyday family life and help your child build a faith that's personal, anchored, and lasting.

This section isn't just about learning more. It's about first letting you as the parent or spiritual guide see why Jesus can truly be the best

Savior for your child so you can extend this confidence and faith to your child.

Also, this will help ensure that Jesus' name is not just a name they've heard, but the One they know they can run to when their questions, fears, and struggles feel overwhelming because He's been where they are right now.

If you want to:

- Get a glimpse of what Jesus' youth was like, **read on.**
- See how Jesus' struggles mirror that of our youth today, **read on.**
- Explore the educational system Jesus was raised in, **read on.**
- Explore the possible educational model for youth today, **read on.**
- See how Jesus' model of formation can point us to ways that can help our children spiritually, **read on.**
- Learn of the practices that filled Jesus' life, **read on.**
- See how Christ overcame the same battles youth face today, **read on.**
- Explore how AI may impact the future for our children, **read on.**
- Learn what it looked like for Jesus to apprentice under godly leaders of His day, His stepfather, and His heavenly father, **read on.**

"For we do not have a high priest who is unable to empathize with our weaknesses, but we have one who has been tempted in every way, just as we are—yet he did not sin."
(Hebrews 4:15)

My Dream...

A Home Distinctly Designed

I had just come from a long journey of serving the youth. I was tired. I sought a safe place. A place to rest. A place I could call home. I went from house to house, person to person, leader to leader, and everywhere I turned, I was not accepted.

Exhausted and heavy-hearted, I returned to Jesus, the One who had sent me on this journey, hoping to find rest.

Rejection after rejection left me without shelter, guidance, and answers. Yet there He was ... Jesus, waiting for me in the basement, quietly anticipating my return.

"Jesus," I cried, overwhelmed. "No one would let me rest for the night. I went from door to door, asking each person if I could stay, and every time, rejection followed. Each place I went, I was shoved away and told to figure it out on my own."

Understanding all too well the plight I faced, Jesus patiently listened to my plea and my cry.

He gently motioned me to the Bible, pointing inside. His eyes held a calm certainty as He spoke:

"Tamara, Tamara, you will never truly fit in these kinds of homes. You are designed to fit only in Me."

Chapter 7

Tempted, Tested, and Twelve

What kid today would ever guess that if they asked Jesus, "Do you even get what I'm going through?" that Jesus would vulnerably respond and say, "I know of these experiences more than you know."

We portray Jesus as this calm, grown-up teacher, and so do our children. We fail to expound on the fact that just like each of us, He had a childhood first. And that childhood wasn't soft or simple.

He grew up dealing with loneliness, side comments, tension in His own home, and the weird pressure of being "different" before He even understood why. He wasn't protected from any of it. He felt the same kind of ache our kids feel when life gets messy, confusing, and unfair. These are all the reasons that makes Him qualified to bear the hardships of our youth.

Honestly, that makes His story hit differently. Jesus' life is relatable. It's close. It's the story of someone who walked through the same emotional fog our kids wade through every day and still grew up to have the strength and power they need now.

Most people in church spaces barely talk about Jesus' childhood. We skip from His birth straight into His ministry like His entire growing-up years were just filler. Other than the story where He goes missing on the family trip, we don't hear much. But those years matter, especially for kids who are trying to figure out who they are.

We tell kids that Jesus is the Son of God, but forget to mention He also had a stepfather. You'd think that little detail would show up more, considering how many kids today are wrestling with blended families and identity questions. We tell them Jesus is their Savior, but we skip over the moment He was so stressed that He sweat blood. That's the part kids in Generation Alpha need to hear, the part that says, "You're not the only one who feels crushed some days." And we teach them how holy Jesus was, but we rarely explain that He was tempted in every way. Kids dealing with sexual temptation, confusion, or pressure desperately need that part spelled out.

If we really want them to hold on to their faith through the ups and downs of life, we can't give them bits and pieces of Jesus' life. They need the whole picture: the beautiful parts, the hard parts, the confusing parts, and the ones we usually skip because they feel too raw.

They need Scripture the way it is, not the cleaned-up version we sometimes hand them. Because Jesus didn't save them from a safe distance. He took wounds, bruises, and rejection on Himself so they could walk in freedom. And when kids understand what He went through, something shifts. They realize He didn't just show up as God, untouched and above it all. He lived inside real human limits. He felt the weight of fear, injustice, loneliness, and pressure, the same stuff they deal with almost every day. And when they see that, it suddenly makes room for their own story too, because they realize they're walking with Someone who has actually felt what they feel and will walk it out with them until they overcome.

Pastor Allen Nolan, in his beautiful sermon titled "*Childhood of Jesus | The Silent Years of Jesus Bible Study,*"[13] walks us through passages most of us skim right past, especially the "silent years" of Jesus' life. It isn't really a history lesson; it is more like someone finally turning the lights on in a room we forgot existed. He explains details buried in Scripture that paint a fuller picture of Jesus' childhood, one most believers never hear growing up.

One of the first things he points out is how Jesus wasn't just living a normal childhood while quietly waiting for adulthood to begin. From a very young age, He carried a spiritual maturity that actually set Him apart. Even His early Bar Mitzvah wasn't just a fun fact; it revealed how deeply connected He already was to His Father. That kind of early devotion might sound beautiful to us, but back then, it made Him stand out more than any kid wants to. It drew attention, questions, and whispers, especially in a community that already had opinions about His birth story deriving from a virgin birth.

The sermon also highlights something that hit a lot harder than expected: Jesus didn't grow up in a warm, unified home. According to the passages the pastor unpacks, His siblings didn't just misunderstand Him. Scripture hints that they rejected Him outright for years. That changes the entire tone of His early life. This wasn't the peaceful Nazareth childhood we imagine. It was a young boy feeling like a stranger in His own family, carrying the weight of who He was without the support of the people who should have loved Him most.

Then came the part nobody talks about: how His goodness itself became the reason He was talked about and mocked. Not because He did anything wrong, but because He refused to bend Himself

[13] Childhood of Jesus | The Silent Years of Jesus Bible Study | Pastor Allen Nolan Sermon https://www.youtube.com/watch?v=z3prHMjY11M&t=109s

to fit the expectations around Him. The sermon describes how the gossip in His small town followed Him for years. Adults joked about Him. Drunks made up cruel rhymes about His mother. Kids repeated what they heard at home. And in all of it, Jesus stayed steady, even when it cost Him His peace, His belonging, and sometimes His safety.

But the pastor doesn't leave it there. He explains the purpose behind it, the part that ties directly into the heart of this chapter: none of Jesus' childhood suffering was accidental. His loneliness, His rejection, His experience of being misunderstood and misjudged, all of it was shaping Him into someone who could truly understand the pain we carry. That's what makes His empathy real, not theoretical. Scripture says He can relate to our weaknesses because He has lived them. The sermon puts language to that truth in a way that's hard to forget.

You can see it in this generation. Teenagers and young adults aren't shy about exploring spiritual practices anymore. They talk about prayer on their feeds, they post their favorite verses, they're open about what they're learning and what still confuses them. There's something sincere about the way they invite their friends along for the ride, like they're all trying to find something solid to stand on in a world that constantly shifts under their feet.

But before any of these practices can actually anchor them, they need to know who they're anchoring themselves to. That's the missing link for a lot of kids. They hear about prayer, the Sabbath, Scripture, Communion, but they don't always hear why Jesus Himself is the safest place to run to. And if they don't know His story, the whole story, then they never really see how deeply He understands everything they're walking through. The identity battles. The mental heaviness. The temptation that creeps in from every direction. Scripture says He was tempted in every way, which means He isn't distant from any of it.

One of the windows into His younger years actually comes from a messianic Psalm[14]. These aren't like the usual Psalms of David where he's venting, confessing, or crying out. Messianic Psalms point straight to Jesus. They describe His experiences long before the New Testament confirms them. When we read them now, it's like opening a door into moments of His childhood and adolescence that the Gospels don't spell out. They help us see the side of Jesus most kids never get told, the side that proves He knows their battles from the inside out.

About 10 percent, or sixteen of the 150 Psalms, are classified as messianic. They are Psalms 2, 8, 16, 22, 23, 24, 40, 41, 45, 68, 69, 72, 89, 102, 110, and 118.

Identity Building of Jesus - Psalm 69: 7-9

7 For I endure scorn for your sake, and shame covers my face. 8 I am a foreigner to my own family, a stranger to my own mother's children; 9 for zeal for your house consumes me, and the insults of those who insult you fall on me.

This verse paints a picture of Jesus' childhood that many people rarely consider. Even as a child, He knew what it was like to feel out of place, to be misunderstood, and even rejected by those closest to

[14] A Messianic Psalm is a Psalm in the Old Testament that is believed to have prophetic content pointing toward the Messiah, Jesus Christ, and his ministry. They often highlight aspects of Jesus' life, death, and resurrection, and are interpreted as foreshadowing his role as the Messiah. Many Messianic Psalms are explicitly quoted and applied to Jesus in the New Testament, further solidifying their Messianic interpretation.

Him. His own siblings didn't believe in Him, and His peers often mocked Him for being different.

Kids today face their own versions of this kind of rejection—being misunderstood at home, at school, or by friends. Jesus' experience shows them that feeling like an outsider is not a flaw; it's part of walking a path that God can use. He endured these challenges and never lost sight of His purpose, giving kids a model for resilience and identity rooted in God, not in the opinions of others.

The Anxiety of Jesus

15 *Do not let the floodwaters engulf me*
or the depths swallow me up
or the pit close its mouth over me.

16 *Answer me, Lord, out of the goodness of your love;*
in your great mercy turn to me.
17 *Do not hide your face from your servant;*
answer me quickly, for I am in trouble.
18 *Come near and rescue me;*
deliver me because of my foes.

19 *You know how I am scorned, disgraced and shamed;*
all my enemies are before you.
20 *Scorn has broken my heart*
and has left me helpless;
I looked for sympathy, but there was none,
for comforters, but I found none.

These verses (Psalm 69: 15-20) give us a real peek into Jesus' feelings. Even as a kid, He had moments of deep worry and felt alone. He knew what it was like to reach out for help and get nothing; His heart carried the weight of being scorned, rejected, and left helpless.

Kids today feel that too, more than we often notice. Pressure from friends, bullying, mental stress, or just feeling invisible can make them feel like they're drowning. Jesus' story shows them that God sees all of it, that being alone sometimes is part of life, and that He truly understands the heaviness of anxiety. It's comforting for kids to know that the One who gets them has been there, felt it, and came through stronger.

Mental Battles - Psalm 69: 9-11

9 for zeal for your house consumes me, and the insults of those who insult you fall on me. 10 When I fast, my enemies mock me; 11 I am the song of the drunkards.

These verses give us a glimpse into Jesus' mental and emotional battles. Even as a young person, He faced ridicule, mockery, and exhaustion from striving to do what was right. He was worn out calling for help, His heart heavy from insults and scorn, and even when He sought God, it felt like no one was there to support Him.

Kids today can connect to this. They face pressure, teasing, and the loneliness of feeling misunderstood or ignored. Just like Jesus, they can feel drained from trying to do the right thing, from fasting, praying, or simply standing up for what they believe in. These verses remind them that their struggles aren't unseen, that Jesus truly understands the weight of mental and emotional battles, and that God is there even when it feels like no one else is.

Sexuality - Psalm 69: 12

12 Those who sit at the gate mock me,
and I am the song of the drunkards.

This verse show just how harshly Jesus was judged, even from a young age. He became the target of gossip and cruel jokes, labeled in ways that could have been deeply shaming: called illegitimate, talked about as a "bastard," and judged for being the son of a stepdad, even though He was born of a virgin.

Kids today can relate to this kind of pressure in their own lives. Whether it's teasing, rumors, or feeling different from peers, the pain of being misunderstood or mocked is real. Seeing that Jesus experienced this kind of social rejection reminds them that they are not alone. God knows the weight of these struggles, and just like Jesus endured and stayed true to His calling, they, too, can navigate the confusing, painful, and often unfair aspects of growing up.

Before we move on from Jesus' childhood, there's something fascinating hidden in Scripture that gives a bigger picture of God's plan. Luke 3 traces Jesus' genealogy all the way back to Adam. Most of us skim these "begats" because they seem like long, boring lists of names—but there's actually a profound message tucked inside. Some Bible teachers, most notably Chuck Missler, have suggested that the traditional meanings of the names listed in Genesis 5 can be arranged into a sentence that reflects the redemptive arc of Scripture.

Each name in Hebrew has a meaning, and when you read the last ten names from Adam to Noah in order, it forms a sentence about God's plan.

> In his book "Cosmic Codes[15]," Missler translated the names in chronological order into English. "Adam - Seth - Enosh - Cainan - Mahalalel - Jared - Enoch - Methuselah - Lamech - Noah" was translated as "Man - (is) Appointed - Mortal - Sorrow; (but) The Blessed God - Shall come down - Teaching - His death shall bring - The Despairing - Comfort or Rest."[16]

[15] Chuck Missler, *Learn the Bible in 24 Hours* (Nashville, TN: Thomas Nelson, 2002), discussion of the genealogy in Genesis 5 and the traditional meanings of the names from Adam to Noah.

[16] https://www.khouse.org/personal_update/articles/2024/son-my-right-hand

Why does this matter for the story we've been telling? Even while Jesus was a child, facing rejection, loneliness, and misunderstanding from the people closest to Him, God's plan was already at work. The hidden message of the genealogy shows that His life, even the hard parts, was part of something bigger. It reminds kids (and adults!) that no matter how confusing or lonely life feels, God sees the whole picture and has a plan that stretches far beyond the struggles of the moment.

This genealogy insight doesn't need to overshadow the real, raw experiences of Jesus' childhood that we've explored in this chapter. It's more like a side note from God: even when life feels lonely or unfair, He's orchestrating something far greater, and His plan is always purposeful, intentional, and full of hope.

So, the whole point of this chapter is that Jesus' childhood wasn't really a fairy tale. He felt lonely, misunderstood, and even rejected by the people who should have loved Him the most.

But here's the thing: every struggle, every moment of scorn and misunderstanding, wasn't wasted. Jesus' pain and isolation were purposeful. They shaped Him into someone who could truly empathize with every human weakness: fear, anxiety, confusion, and even the temptations our kids face today. When He looked at the world, He didn't see it from a distance; He felt it from the inside, and that makes His love and guidance for our youth incredibly real and accessible.

For kids today, this is a game-changer. Social pressures, bullying, mental stress, and the confusion that comes with identity or faith struggles can feel overwhelming. But Jesus' life is proof that feeling unseen, lonely, or misunderstood doesn't have to define the journey. He understands it all, down to the deepest, quietest hurts.

So, as we guide our children, as we teach them about Scripture and faith, it's not just about knowledge or rules, it isn't even a certain direction, destination, or demographic location ... it's about connection. Connection to a God who knows their hearts, who's walked their path, and who's ready to meet them right where they are. It's about the only answer that exists for a wailing heart. It is The Way. The Truth. The Light.

They're not alone in their struggles. Jesus walked that road first, and His life shows them they can endure, grow, and find hope, even in the moments that feel darkest.

That's the invitation of His story: to let our kids see a Savior who gets it, who's been there, and who will never leave them. And when they grasp that, faith becomes more than something to learn, it becomes something they can live, carry, and rely on for a lifetime.

"I am the way and the truth and the life.
No one comes to the Father except through me."
(John 14:6)

My Dream...

Learn of Me

It had been a long, hard journey for me. After seasons of exclusion, rejection, and pain, I now found myself standing in the back of a large, old warehouse, surrounded by a sea of people. I wondered, "Why am I here? What is this gathering? Who are all these people?" Low, scattered conversations filled the air, mixed with the familiar sounds and smells of the building.

Then, suddenly, everything went quiet. So quiet you could hear a pin drop. The presence of the Lord filled the room. The crowd seemed to part, with half of the people moving to the left and the other half to the right, creating a wide aisle down the center of the warehouse. I stood frozen, watching, trying to understand what was happening.

Then the Lord motioned for me to walk down the middle. I couldn't move. The silence felt heavy. A second time, He called me forward.

Slowly, with trembling steps, I began to walk down the long aisle toward the front. No one spoke. All eyes were fixed ahead. As I kept my focus on Jesus, strength rose up within me. He became the power that carried me forward, step by step, until I finally reached the front.

Chapter 8

The Way Jesus Learned

Up to this point, we've spent time sitting with the harder parts of Jesus' early life. We've looked at His loneliness, His rejection, and the quiet suffering that shaped His childhood long before the cross. That matters, because kids today are carrying heavy things too. Identity questions. Anxiety. Feeling unseen. Feeling different. If Jesus truly understands them, then His story has to reach further back than adulthood and public ministry.

But there's another question that naturally follows all of this. If Jesus grew up facing so much pain, misunderstanding, and pressure, how did He become who He was? How did a child marked by rejection grow into a man filled with peace, authority, compassion, and strength? Hardship alone doesn't form a soul. Some may say, "Well He was the son of God, and His assignment was to overcome so that we could look to Him as a reliable source and so could our children." Something else must have been at work beneath the surface.

This chapter looks at that "something else." It steps into the educational and formative world Jesus grew up in and explores how He was shaped, taught, and grounded as a child. Not just in a classroom sense, but in the deeper sense of formation. As we take a closer look at what learning, apprenticeship, and spiritual training looked like in Jesus' culture, we begin to see how His inner life was built. And in doing so, we gain insight into what helps children today not just survive their struggles but grow through them.

Gaining a glimpse of the hardship Jesus faced as a youth, draws children closer to Him because they realize He truly understands what they are going through. Knowing that loneliness, abandonment, and questions of identity were part of His early life gives kids a reason to lean in and listen to what He has to say about overcoming. As we explore what Jesus' education looked like on the surface and what was happening beneath it, we begin to uncover the foundation that supported His life, His faith, and His ability to endure.

Before we go into the educational system that Jesus was a part of, let's take a glimpse at history, as well as the present and projected education of this young generation.

Today Generation Alpha spends seven to eight hours per day in a classroom. In the early 1800s, education in our country was more of a model of apprenticeship where once children learned the basics of reading, writing, and arithmetic in early childhood, they would study under a skilled leader like an engineer, doctor, writer, or builder in order to build their future.

In 1843, Horace Mann returned to America from Europe to share the "Prussian model of education," a school model designed to create factory workers and what most Americans call school today. Just as this model of education can no longer be fitting for a generation growing with the progress of artificial intelligence (AI), the way we teach spiritual formation will not be sufficient for an anchored and lasting faith in our children.

In the book, *Open Education* by Matt Bowman and Isaac Morehouse, it is projected that educational models like apprenticeship, prevalent in our early history will become one of the models that will build future leaders in our country because of the overtaking of AI.

AI expert, Dr. Roman Yampolskly, projects that by 2030 over 90 percent of the promising careers familiar throughout our history will be eliminated. Generation Alpha is in a unique disposition where the futures that once existed will be a new world for everyone including them.

The educational model, once designed for workers and not leaders, will no longer be fitting for our children. Apprenticeship has already begun to spring up as one of the future models of education. It isn't new and has proven success in many economic cultures. This is the model of education Jesus grew up in, and not only did it instruct Him academically, but it formed Him spiritually. It can do the same for our children. Luke 2:40 states, "And the child grew, and waxed strong in spirit, filled with wisdom: and the grace of God was upon him."

Let's dive into Jesus' formative years and peer into what that world looked like.

Jesus and the Way He Was Formed

Imagine a world without the framework of sitting in a classroom for seven to eight hours. One where open discussion was the platform for knowledge. A world where children sat with scholars for their formation and learned under the good leadership. One where plants and science were not studied in textbooks but in the outdoors. Imagine a world where rush was not the norm, but rest was the culture. A world where relationships were the foundation for routine. This is a small picture of what Jesus' world looked like.

Much of what we understand about Jesus' early formation comes from the first-century Jewish educational system, a world very different from ours, yet surprisingly relevant. Some of this framework is drawn from historical teaching models described in *Practicing the Way* (pp. 7–8), with added reflection on how this shaped Jesus personally and how it can shape our children today.

From a young age, Jesus would have been part of a synagogue-based elementary school. Around age five, Jewish children began formal learning, not centered on creativity or self-expression as we define it today, but on immersion in Scripture. Children learned to read, write, and memorize the Torah, the first five books of the Bible. By the time they were twelve or thirteen, many had the entire Torah memorized.

In our culture, that kind of spiritual discipline would be celebrated as extraordinary, almost unbelievable. In Jewish culture, it was considered basic. This was the starting line, not the finish. Memorizing Genesis through Deuteronomy meant you were minimally educated, not elite.

Jesus would have been among these children. He knew Scripture deeply. Yet unlike many of His peers, He also carried profound emotional weight. He lived with the trauma of rejection, the confusion of being misunderstood, and the awareness that His Father was not earthly but divine. That awareness didn't isolate Him from humanity; it anchored Him to it. It made Him both vulnerable and deeply empathetic.

After age twelve or thirteen, most children ended their formal education. They returned home to apprentice in the family trade such as carpentry, farming, tax collecting, or metalwork. Education, as we think of it, was done.

Jesus followed this path outwardly. He apprenticed under Joseph as a carpenter. But inwardly, His deepest apprenticeship was under His Father in heaven.

Only a small number of students continued beyond this stage. Those who showed exceptional ability entered a higher level of learning called *midrash*, the house of learning. By their mid to late teens, these students would have memorized much of the rest of the Hebrew

Scriptures. Even then, many went on to marry, start families, and live ordinary lives.

From this already small group, an even smaller number was selected by rabbis to apprentice under them directly. This was the highest honor. The goal was not just knowledge but transformation to become like the rabbi in thought, action, character, and authority.

This process was intense. Rabbis tested candidates relentlessly. They questioned their understanding, discipline, and endurance. Only those who proved exceptional were invited with a simple but life-altering call: "Come, follow me."

To follow meant total immersion. The apprentice left behind family expectations, familiar routines, and personal ambition. They ate what the rabbi ate, walked where he walked, and listened constantly. They learned not just what he taught, but how he lived. The goal was to have such a complete transformation that others could recognize who your rabbi was simply by watching you.

Eventually, the apprentice would be sent out to repeat the process, inviting others to follow and be formed in the same way.

This matters deeply for our children today.

Jesus did not rise out of His childhood wounds by accident. His authority, peace, obedience, and love were formed through a life of intentional apprenticeship. He learned how to carry suffering without being consumed by it. He learned how to remain grounded in truth while surrounded by misunderstanding. He learned how to love without belonging.

Our children carry emotional burdens heavier than we often realize. Yet just like Jesus, they are not meant to carry them alone. The same God who formed Christ through hardship is also present to form our children today. There is a path from pain to purpose, from confusion to clarity, and from rejection to belonging.

And that path does not begin with perfection. It begins with formation.

Jesus walked it first. Now He invites our children to walk it with Him.

When the Way Is a Person, Not a Formula

We all want a formula—something simple we can follow that guarantees our kids will grow up with a strong, lasting faith. We want to say the right things, teach the right lessons, and put them in the right programs. But faith does not work like a recipe. Children are not machines, and transformation is not mechanical.

A lasting faith in Jesus has never been about a formula. Instead, it has been about relationship. Scripture reminds us that God is Spirit, and those who worship Him must worship in spirit and in truth. That alone tells us something important. Faith is not transferred through information alone. It is formed through lived connection.

Jesus Himself grew up surrounded by the educational systems and cultural expectations of His time, yet His deepest formation did not come from institutions. It came from trust and from walking closely with His Father in heaven. His life shows us what happens when earthly experience and heavenly relationship meet in one human life.

If the youngest generation is going to experience Jesus in a real and lasting way, they need more than reassurance that He understands their struggles. They need to see *how* He was formed through them. How a childhood marked by rejection, misunderstanding, and pressure became a life marked by peace, authority, love, obedience, and strength. And the adults who walk with them must understand this path too, because it changes how we guide, teach, and support them.

Jesus' ultimate Rabbi was not a human one. While others apprenticed under imperfect, demanding, and often rigid teachers, Jesus apprenticed under God Himself. And what He encountered was not cold discipline, but love.

Jesus did not have to earn being chosen. He was known and chosen before the foundations of the world. What He had to do was learn how to live in a broken world within a human body. And He did not do that alone. He did it in constant relationship with the One who knew Him fully.

Instead of a rabbi who drilled Him with questions and tests, Jesus learned to face life's challenges through the lens of love. Instead of absorbing the habits of a mortal teacher, He learned the ways, thoughts, tone, and heart of an eternal God. He learned how God listens, how God responds, and how God loves.

Jesus learned to ask questions, to listen, to sit with sinners, to eat with those on the margins, and to love people the way God loves people. His strength did not come from isolation. It came from closeness. His safety did not come from avoidance of pain. It came from being with God in the middle of it.

Over time, Jesus embodied that relationship so fully that others were drawn to Him. And when the time came, He did what all true apprentices eventually do. He invited others to follow, to walk with Him, and to be formed the same way.

This is what following Jesus has always meant. Not just learning about Him, but learning *from* Him. Not imitation from a distance, but immersion up close.

Our youth are not designed to simply be told who Jesus is, or even to copy His behavior. They are designed to discover who they are *in Him*. In Hebrew thought, a disciple, a *talmid*, was not a student collecting information, but a practitioner living an embodied way of life.

Western culture often pushes the opposite. More data. More noise. More pressure. Less rest. Less reflection. Less space to listen. In Jesus' world, wisdom mattered more than information. Formation mattered more than performance.

To follow Jesus meant to walk beside Him, listen to Him, observe Him, obey Him, and slowly become like Him. Discipleship was not something done *to* you. It was something that happened *through* you as you yielded your life to God.

Unlike many leaders of His time, Jesus led with love. And love remains the true test of spiritual formation. His invitation was not simply to become better people, but to enter into the inner life of God Himself.

Our children carry burdens that often feel heavier than adults realize. Mental pressure. Sexual confusion. Identity struggles. Overwhelm. Jesus faced these battles too, and He overcame them not by escaping humanity, but by walking it with God.

He did not have an ordinary rabbi. And neither do our kids.

They have an invitation to walk with the same Father, the same presence, and the same love that formed Jesus Himself.

Ancient Biblical Practices for Youth

So, the question we have to ask is this: *What actually formed a child like Jesus?*

What were the rhythms, practices, and daily ways of living that carried Him through confusion, rejection, pressure, and pain, and still shaped Him into someone anchored, whole, and deeply connected to God?

Jesus did not grow up with modern resources, therapy language, or structured youth programs. Yet somehow, in the middle of hardship and misunderstanding, His life remained grounded, purposeful, and free. That tells us something important. His strength did not come from avoiding struggle. It came from the practices that kept Him connected to the Father.

This section looks closely at those ancient biblical practices, not as religious routines, but as living pathways—practices that shaped Jesus as a child and young adult, and practices that can still shape our children today.

Nine practices were intentionally chosen and grouped around three areas where youth today are struggling the most: identity, mental wellness, and sexuality. These areas are not abstract issues. They show up in real lives, real questions, and real pain. The practices were not selected randomly, but because they directly speak to these struggles in a way that is both biblical and deeply human.

The nine practices include biblical meditation, Socratic conversation, reading Scripture in context, epistle writing, worship, sabbath rest, prayer, Communion, and participation in small, intimate, intergenerational groups.

What makes these practices effective is not just that they are ancient or biblical, but that they are participatory, engaging, and connect kids to God in a kinesthetic and spiritual way. They invite youth to engage, reflect, question, rest, listen, and respond. Faith is not something they are told to accept. It is something they are invited to live into.

Within the area of identity, practices like Communion, worship, epistle writing, and sabbath rest help youth reconnect with who they are and whose they are. These practices slow them down, root them in belonging, and remind them that identity is received, not earned.

For emotional wellness, practices such as biblical meditation, prayer, and small intergenerational groups create space for stillness, honesty, and support. They address anxiety, loneliness, and overwhelm not by numbing them, but by holding them in the presence of God and safe community.

In the area of sexuality, Socratic conversation and reading Scripture in context allow youth to ask real questions without fear. Instead of shame or silence, these practices create room for clarity, wisdom, and truth grounded in love.

When we look at the life of Jesus, we see these same practices woven naturally throughout His story. Although He was among the chosen few, His apprenticeship was not limited to the spiritual leaders of His time or even to His stepfather's trade. His deepest formation came through His relationship with His Heavenly Father.

Jesus had already completed an apprenticeship under His stepfather as a carpenter, learning how to work with His hands, show up daily, and live faithfully in ordinary life. But alongside that, His entire life was marked by practices that continually bridged Him back to God.

We see Him engaging in deep, thoughtful conversations about the Torah, asking questions and dialoguing with scholars. We see Him in safe, intimate, intergenerational spaces with people like Mary, Martha, and even Zacchaeus, where honest and difficult conversations were welcomed. We see Him walking through fields on the Sabbath, slowing down, resting, and teaching His disciples along the way. We see Him overwhelmed to the point of sweating drops of blood, and yet choosing surrender instead of escape. We see

Him meditating on God's Word before facing temptation. We hear Him crying out to the Father with raw emotion. And we are left with His Words, His teachings, and His letters to us through Scripture.

These were not isolated spiritual moments. They were a way of life.

Jesus lived these practices so our children would have a way back. A way to reconnect with a God who is not distant or disappointed, but loving and present; and a God who understands their struggles and is still calling them home.

Scripture states, "And the child grew, and waxed strong in spirit, filled with wisdom: and the grace of God was upon him" (Luke 2:40). Jesus' childhood was a critical part of His journey. His earthly life ended in His thirties. After enduring a difficult youth, I am sure His young adult years before ministry held much that could benefit us, but what is most significant for our children is what happened between His crucifixion and His ascension back to heaven.

Jesus' body was marked with everything that represents the needs our children carry today. The crown of thorns, in many ways, reflects the mental agony the enemy places on our kids. He was lifted on a cross, exposed to the eyes of the world in nakedness, humiliation, and scorn. This mirrors the shame first seen in the garden when Adam and Eve became aware of their nakedness and experienced sexual brokenness. He cried out to His Father, yet in that moment He was not answered, because He had become the sin we had committed, and God could not look upon sin. In a very real sense, God was exchanging the weight of our children's sin for their salvation. Yet the story of redemption did not end at the cross. What followed next revealed just how far Christ was willing to go to break the power of sin and darkness.

Jesus went to hell. Yes, He went to hell and faced the hell our children go through, so they could exchange their sin for His life.

For three days and three nights He faced the enemy and overcame him, winning the battle over sin once and for all.

Then God's power raised Him from the dead, and He appeared again to His disciples, His friends, and His family.

What He said to them next is especially important for understanding how our youth are meant to be supported today. He explained that He had to go so that the Helper could come. "But very truly I tell you, it is for your good that I am going away. Unless I go away, the Advocate will not come to you; but if I go, I will send him to you." (John 16).

Biblical Meditation

Biblical meditation is one of the most misunderstood practices in modern Christianity. We often rush Scripture. We read to finish, not to dwell on it. But Jesus didn't interact with God's Word that way. Scripture lived inside Him. It shaped His instincts, His responses, and His courage in moments of testing.

When Jesus was tempted, He didn't scramble for answers. Scripture flowed out of Him because it had already been flowing *into* Him for years. He had learned to sit with God's Word long enough for it to become part of Him.

For children, biblical meditation invites them to slow down in a world that never stops talking. Sitting with a short passage, reading it carefully, asking honest questions, and reflecting on what it means for their own life helps Scripture move from being something they hear about to something they actually experience. Over time, this practice builds patience, imagination, and spiritual resilience. It teaches kids that God speaks personally, not just generally.

Socratic Conversation

Jesus rarely lectured people into transformation. Instead, He asked questions. He invited conversation. He allowed people to discover truth rather than forcing it upon them. This was especially true when dealing with brokenness, shame, and sexuality.

When Jesus spoke with the woman at the well, Mary and Martha, or the woman who washed His feet with her tears, He did not lead with condemnation. He led with curiosity, compassion, and truth. His questions opened doors that shame had closed.

Socratic conversation allows youth to engage Scripture and difficult topics without fear. Rather than being told what to think, they are invited to explore *why* God responds the way He does. This is incredibly important when addressing sexuality. When kids are given space to ask honest questions and wrestle with Scripture in a safe environment, they learn that Jesus is not afraid of their curiosity or their struggle.

Epistle Writing

Letters in Scripture were deeply personal. Paul's letters to Timothy weren't distant theological essays; they were words soaked in love, encouragement, and belief. Paul spoke identity into Timothy long before Timothy fully saw it in himself.

Jesus, too, left words meant to be returned to again and again. His teachings were not just for the moment; they were anchors for the future.

Epistle writing gives youth a tangible way to speak life into one another. Writing letters of encouragement allows kids to slow down and reflect on what God is doing in their own hearts and in the lives of others. For youth struggling with identity, receiving written affirmation rooted in faith can become something they return to during moments of doubt. It becomes a physical reminder that they are seen, known, and valued.

Worship

Worship did not begin with music. It began with surrender. From the earliest stories in Scripture, worship was about offering God one's best, not one's performance. Jesus lived this truth daily. His entire life was oriented toward honoring the Father.

Helping youth understand worship as more than singing reshapes how they relate to God. Worship becomes less about emotion and more about attachment. It teaches kids to let go of self-focus and reorient their hearts toward who God is. When worship is practiced this way, it becomes a powerful place of freedom rather than pressure.

Sabbath Rest

Sabbath rest is one of the most radical practices Jesus honored. Rest directly confronts the lie that worth is earned through constant activity. From the beginning of creation, God showed that identity comes before productivity.

For youth, sabbath rest can feel uncomfortable at first. Stopping feels threatening in a culture that ties value to performance. But practicing sabbath rest gently teaches children that they are loved before they achieve anything. It invites them to rest in God's presence and discover an identity rooted in grace rather than striving. Over time, sabbath rest becomes a healing rhythm that anchors the soul.

Prayer

Jesus prayed constantly. Sometimes quietly. Sometimes with tears. Sometimes with loud cries. Prayer was not polished or performative. It was honest and relational. It was where Jesus brought His fear, trust, confusion, and surrender to the Father.

Teaching youth how to pray this way gives them language for their inner world. Prayer becomes a place where anxiety can be named, trust can be rebuilt, and hope can be restored. It reminds them that they are not meant to carry life alone.

Text in Context

Scripture without context can feel harsh or confusing, especially when addressing sexuality. Jesus consistently revealed the heart behind God's commands. He showed that boundaries were rooted in love and protection, not punishment.

Teaching youth to read Scripture in context helps them understand *why* God speaks the way He does. When kids learn the historical and cultural background of difficult passages, they begin to trust God's heart instead of pulling away from it. Context transforms fear into understanding.

Communion

Communion brings faith into the body. Jesus invited His followers to remember Him not just with thoughts, but through participation. Bread and cup became reminders of His love, sacrifice, and presence.

For youth, Communion offers a sacred pause. A moment to name struggles, remember Christ's sacrifice, and receive grace again. It reminds them that their battles were not ignored by Jesus, but carried by Him.

Small Intergenerational Groups

Jesus lived life in close relational spaces. Mary, Martha, Lazarus, and Zacchaeus—these were places of safety, honesty, and belonging. They were environments where questions were welcomed and vulnerability was met with love.

Small intergenerational groups offer youth something deeply formative: one trusted adult, one safe space, and one consistent relationship. These environments allow faith to grow naturally and deeply. Often, transformation happens not in large gatherings, but in quiet conversations where a child feels seen and heard.

* * *

To sum it all up, it's easy to look at our kids and think the answer to their struggles is just another rule, program, or some step-by-step formula. But what we've seen in Jesus' life tells a different story. The real answer is always a Person, and walking with Him is a path, it's not some checklist. See, Jesus didn't escape the hardships of childhood; He faced them, and yet He grew up whole, strong, and anchored in love because He lived in constant relationship with His Father. Every practice, every moment of apprenticeship, and every rhythm of His life shaped Him from the inside out. And the amazing thing is, these same practices, worship, prayer, meditation, sabbath rest, conversation, Communion, and small, safe communities, can help our children navigate their own struggles today. They're not just old traditions; they are bridges connecting a child's heart back to the God who is waiting for them. As we close this chapter, keep in mind that the path Jesus walked is not distant history … it's a living way for kids to grow in faith, identity, and resilience, and it's a journey we get to guide them through.

My Dream...

The Good Shepherd

Anyone who knows me well knows that I don't do strange animals or unfamiliar dogs very well. I'm allergic to a lot of fur, and honestly, I've never been comfortable with animals that jump on you or lick you without warning. In this dream, it was clear that Jesus knew that about me.

I found myself walking along a path when suddenly a fierce, threatening creature appeared, almost as if it had been assigned to stop me from reaching where I was going. It growled loudly, baring its teeth, trying to intimidate me. I froze. Fear rushed through my body, and I felt completely unable to move. I had no way to defend myself, and I truly believed I was alone with this thing.

Then, out of nowhere, Jesus appeared. In His hand was a simple thread. He wrapped it calmly around the creature's neck. It was such a small thing, yet it completely restrained it. Then He motioned for me to keep walking, to pass right through the very path the enemy had been blocking.

I stepped forward hesitantly. The creature still wanted to attack me, but it couldn't. It was powerless against that thread Jesus held. And I realized, even in my fear, that what tried to stop me had no authority once He had taken hold of it.

Chapter 9

The Jesus Our Kids Never Met

While it seems that our youth struggle to connect with Jesus, it is because we have fed them a version of Jesus that cannot relate to where they are. Jesus is their defense, their advocate, and their deliverer from fears, traps, and enemies that seem to be consuming them. Our youth must be allowed to learn not only of the powerful version of who Christ is, but also of the mild version that is tender enough to comfort them as a mother would her child during crisis moments (Isaiah 66:13).

The stories in the Bible were never meant to be edited down for Generation Alpha. They were meant to be entered into. When young people are invited to step inside these moments, to wrestle with the questions, the tension, and the emotions, they begin to take ownership of their faith. This is the same way Jesus learned, through honest conversation, deep reflection, and lived experience, whether it was the searching questions He asked in the temple at twelve years old, the meditation Joshua practiced to gain courage, or the personal letters Timothy received to strengthen his faith.

What you're about to read is written a little differently on purpose. These devotionals are written in the first person so you can step inside the story and see what was happening beneath the surface. Instead of just reading what Jesus or others did, you're invited to feel the pressure, doubt, fear, and surrender that came with it. This is the same way Jesus taught, through conversation, questions, and reflection, not just rules. It's how Joshua found courage through meditation, and how Timothy found strength through personal letters when he felt discouraged.

As you read, remember this isn't meant to replace Scripture or change it. It's meant to guide our youth alongside it. These reflections invite you into moments of identity struggle, mental battles, and hard questions about sexuality so that our youth can envision how faith speaks directly into the same places they wrestle with today. What follows are examples of what it looks like when faith is not just taught, but lived, felt, and honestly worked through.

When Jesus faced an Identity Crisis

Jesus—A Challenge to My Identity (Matthew 4:1–11)

It felt like death was standing right outside the door. I had been fasting for forty days in the wilderness, searching for God's will, trying to listen. My body was worn down. My skin was dry. My stomach was empty. I felt weak, almost hollow, like I couldn't hold myself up anymore. And yet, somehow, even in that state, God was holding me.

My strength was gone, but my spirit was still awake. Sharp. Alert. That's when the temptation started showing up from every direction. I wanted food more than anything. I wanted relief. I wanted to feel strong again. I also wanted to walk in power, to move with authority, and to show what I carried. But instead of rising, I collapsed. I sank to the ground and buried my face in my hands.

And then it got harder.

The Spirit had led me into the wilderness to be tested by the devil. The wilderness wasn't comforting. It was dry. Empty. Lifeless. Worse than the valley. And that's where temptation was waiting. I barely had the strength to stand when the enemy showed up, asking questions, circling me, setting traps. Every question was aimed at shrinking me, pulling me away from who God said I was. I had never felt more exposed, more vulnerable. Honestly, it felt like the perfect moment to fail.

The first thing he said was, "If you are really the Son of God, why don't you turn these stones into bread?"

And yes, I was starving. Every part of me wanted to prove who I was. To use my power. To show it. One hit came straight at my identity, another at my worth. I wrestled with it. I could do it. But I wasn't authorized to. And I knew that stepping into power without the Father's direction would drop me right where the enemy wanted me. Have you ever been dared to prove yourself? Pressured to act out of character just to be believed? That's what was happening. The words I had been storing in my heart rose up. I used what little strength I had left and said, "Man does not live by bread alone, but by every word that comes from God." That response took everything out of me. Or so I thought.

He wasn't finished.

While I remained weak and dizzy, he led me to the highest point of the temple and said, "If you are the Son of God, jump. The Scriptures say God will send angels to catch you." Honestly, I didn't need to jump. I felt like I might fall on my own. The implication was clear. End it. Prove it. Force God's hand. Again, I pulled from what I knew and said, "It is also written: do not test God."

Then came the final push.

He took me to a high mountain and showed me the kingdoms of the world. The beauty. The power. The glory. And he said if I would bow to him, it could all be mine. The irony was heavy. It already belonged to my Father. And to me. But not that way. Not through compromise. Not through worshipping the wrong thing. I was exhausted, starving, worn down by lies. I finally said, "Get out of my face. I will worship God and God alone. You have no authority here."

It had been a long day. I was empty. Shaken. But when the enemy left, God sent His angels. Not because I tested Him, but because I obeyed Him. The devil had nothing left to grab onto.

Even at my weakest, God never left me. He let me walk through the testing, but He stayed close the whole time. He watched it unfold. And He carried me through.

When Jesus Faced a emotional Crisis

Jesus—A Challenge to My Emotional Crisis (Luke 22:41-44)

I had just finished sharing some deeply personal things with my closest friends. Things about what was coming. Things I didn't want to face alone. I asked three of them to walk with me to the olive presses nearby. I needed to get away from the noise of the marketplace, the constant movement, the pressure of being seen. The garden was quiet. People went there to rest, to breathe, and to step away. That's what I needed most. I needed support. I needed to not feel so alone in what I was about to face.

As soon as we arrived, a heavy wave of sorrow hit me. It came out of nowhere and all at once. I was overwhelmed. I had hoped being with my friends would steady me, but the battle had already started inside my mind.

I tried to quiet myself so I could talk to my Father, but the sorrow only grew heavier. I finally said out loud, "I feel like I'm about to die." I begged them to stay close, to stay awake, to watch over me. "Can you just sit and pray with me for one hour?" I didn't need advice. I didn't need fixing. I just needed presence. I needed someone to stand with me. But this was a battle no one else could fight for me.

I walked farther into the garden and collapsed. My face hit the ground as I cried out. My soul ached. "Dad … please … take this darkness away from me." The weight was unbearable. My thoughts were chaotic, pulling me in every direction. *I don't want to do this. I do want to do this. I can't. I don't know how. God, help me. Rescue me.* I had nothing left. The fight was too much. So, I let go. I surrendered. "Not my plan. Yours."

The weight of the world pressed down on me. Every sin. Every failure. Every broken life. My body reacted to the war happening inside me. I was sweating heavily, and when I wiped my face, I saw blood on my hands. I was under so much stress that my body was breaking under it. I was at the edge of death.

After surrendering, I went back to the friends I trusted the most. I needed them. I couldn't believe what I saw. One was completely asleep. Another was barely conscious, snoring loudly. The third was drooling like he'd been out for hours. "Hey!" I cried out. "Couldn't you stay awake and pray with me for just one hour?"

Even my closest friends couldn't stay with me in my weakest moment. I reminded them, "You need to pray so you don't give in. Your spirit is willing, but your flesh is weak."

As I stood there, I thought about you. About everyone who would one day experience the love of my Father because of what I was about to endure. Because of the shame I would carry, you would have a way back to God. That hope. That joy. That kept me going. That's how I endured the cross. And I did it for you.

The Testimony of the Believer

Each of these testimonies is a result of the death Jesus endured on the cross. His death was for our children and for us. Jesus clearly stated that the Kingdom of God is built up by children. Yet few in

Generation Alpha is growing up to know God. They are also the first generation being raised by the highest rate of parents who do not believe; and among those being raised by those who do believe, the effort to make faith a priority is often casual and ritualistic instead of intentional.

When the Answer Leaves Us a Comforter

Jesus ended up growing into full maturity, journeying closely with God and man. (Luke 2:52) He ended up loving both God and man so very deeply that He died a gruesome death on a wretched cross. For our sake, He took our burdens and bore every sin that we and our children could ever imagine or experience.

Because He was born of a virgin through the conception from God Himself, this made Him the candidate that could eradicate our ongoing battles with sin and gain the victory for us to do the same. Jesus was bullied, spat on, hung naked, teased, and endured all the temptations we face, yet He was not found with sin.

He experienced the mental battles faced by our children and tempted at all points of sexual sin but never yielded. Nonetheless, we find Christ becoming a full, fledge ball of sin, hanging on the cross so that we would not experience the damnation promised to all who sin and fall short of the glory of God. What's more is that He proved victory by fighting the crude enemy of every man's soul that has ever lived. He fought the enemy that torments our children on a regular basis and won victory over this evil force.

He rose up from death and returned to let His people know that He is alive and well and forever makes fervent prayers on our behalf as we trust in Him. Not only is He doing this for us and our children today, but before leaving Earth, He left a comforter named, the Holy Spirit. He clearly stated this in John 16:7 where He said, "It is to your advantage that I go away. If I do not go away then the Helper will not come to you. If I go, I will send Him to you."

As the loneliest generation that's ever lived, we must remind our kids that the Holy Spirit is always an ever-present help in time of need, and He will never leave them nor forsake them. Our children can be so comfortable with the concept of imaginary friends. If they can perceive this, they can be confident that they are never alone as the reality of God being present is more real, true, and transformative than friends of the imagination. Let us leave them with these truths—Emmanuel, God is with us.

Closing Reflections –The Answer

At that moment the curtain of the temple was torn in two from top to bottom. The earth shook, the rocks split.
Matthew 27:51

Jewish historian Josephus often cited the miraculous nature of the curtain tearing at Jesus' crucifixion. While Josephus describes the veil as four inches thick and immense, many commentaries indicate it would take the power of twelve strong horses to rip the veil apart.

One of the greatest spiritual struggles for all humanity before the appearance of Christ was the barrier between man and God. This barrier existed because of sin. God could not allow sin in His presence. The day that Jesus died on the cross, He became sin even though He did not commit any sin. As soon as Jesus died, the curtain that separated man and God in the Old Testament was ripped. All humanity had the freedom to see who God was without any barriers. The endless and bountiful love of God was now made clear. No longer did individuals have to go through the priest to get to God or fulfill many sacrifices. Jesus became the ultimate sacrifice.

Today, our children can come boldly to God and have face-to-face encounters with Him. Our children have information about God at their fingertips but what they are in need of is Biblical encounters that transcend book knowledge and nourish their spiritual thirst.

This is why Jesus came. He came to seek and save those who are lost in a world full of superficial promises.

Jesus came to be the answer to every question our kids would ask like, "Why do I feel lonely? Why is anxiety such a struggle within me? Why is sexuality so confusing? Why do I feel the need to have someone close to me all the time?"

To find these answers, our children must become acquainted with Christ not only through His sacrifice on the cross but as a human who walked through many of the things that they face today. As youth journey through the human struggle Jesus faced, they can begin to see Him as their answer and as their Lord and Savior.

The childhood of Jesus and the stories of people who followed are meant to show what real transformation looks like when Generation Alpha is guided to follow God fully. Life isn't always neat or comfortable, and the practices Jesus lived were ways He connected to His Father on a regular basis. His cries to God proved to be authentic, raw, and transformative.

For young believers, these examples show that even when the world pulls in a hundred directions, even when their bodies, minds, or habits tempt them to take shortcuts, God still provides a way through. He does not leave them alone in the struggle. There is hope and guidance., as well as a life of purpose waiting when they lean into Him and into the disciplines that form a lasting connection with God.

God's answer is not so much the problems Jesus faced as a youth or adult, but the power He carried within to overcome them. With that, He had a lifestyle of practices that connected Him to His Father. Our children can grow in their relationship with God in the same way.

It is essential for our youth to know that we have a High Priest who is able to relate to their griefs and struggles. He is deeply acquainted with them. He was tempted in every way they are, yet without sin. Because of this, they can trust Him, believe His Word, and know that the same power that enabled Him to overcome is available to help them overcome as well.

PART III

DAILY PRACTICES FOR YOUTH

Section Preview

In Part One, we listened to "The Cry." Then in Part Two, we were introduced to "The Answer." In this final section, we learn how to walk with that answer in everyday life through "Practices."

Knowing who Jesus is and what He overcame is powerful, but our children must have a conscious awareness of Him in their everyday lives. They need to know how to stay connected to Him in the middle of their real, daily battles. More than information, they need encounters with God. More than inspiration, they need rhythms, habits, and sacred practices that help them experience God as close, personal, and present through the power of the Holy Spirit.

Practices do not replace God, and they are not empty rituals. They are bridges. They are the ways our earthly lives learn to stay in step with an invisible, yet very real, Savior. These are the same practices Jesus Himself lived—ways of listening, resting, praying, reflecting, remembering, and belonging—that anchored Him to the Father and can now anchor our children in a world that constantly pulls them in every direction.

Many of these practices have either been misunderstood, watered down, or quietly forgotten. Meditation is often confused with emptying the mind instead of filling it with God's Word. Communion is reduced to a quick ritual instead of a moment of deep connection, repentance, forgiveness, and belonging. Yet when practiced with understanding and intention, these rhythms become powerful meeting places between our children and the heart of God.

In this section, the practices are grouped around the very areas where Generation Alpha is struggling most: identity, mental and emotional battles, and sexuality. While these practices can be integrated across different struggles, I have grouped them according to the areas where they respond with the greatest impact.

The goal is simple but sacred: to offer our children practical, lived-out pathways to know God, hear His voice, feel His closeness, and grow roots deep enough to withstand the pressures of the world around them.

In Genesis 28:10–19, we see a powerful example of what follows the practice of intentional engagement with God. Jacob leaves his country to follow his father's instructions. As he endures a long journey while escaping danger, he pauses to rest. In doing so, he finds a few rocks and lays his head upon them. As he falls asleep, Jacob has a dream that shifts not only his spiritual journey but the trajectory of his life.

Jacob dreams of a ladder anchored on earth that reaches up into heaven. On this ladder, heavy spiritual activity takes place as angels travel back and forth between heaven and earth, again and again.

Jacob is amazed by the activity occurring in the spiritual realm on behalf of humanity. He is astonished to discover that God is actively involved in the affairs of humankind.

After waking from his dream, Jacob declares that the place will be called the House of God. He then vows that if God leads him safely to his destination, he will serve and worship God all the days of his life.

When our children engage in practices that connect them to Christ, they will be able to easily recognize when God is in their midst.

Nothing in this life could rival the encounters they build through engaging with God and experiencing Him for themselves. Once Jacob saw God, there was no turning back to his old ways. He had glimpsed a spiritual dimension that was utterly real, one intimately acquainted with the people of the earth, and that includes our children.

Practices that engage children with God serve as pathways that lead to permanence in a lasting relationship with Him.

In this section, daily biblical practices will be discussed, along with how these practices can be incorporated into children's everyday lives.

If you want to:

- Learn the daily practices that will support the spiritual development of children in the areas of identity, mental wellness, and sexuality, **read on.**
- Apply the ancient biblical practices that flourished individuals spiritually in biblical history, **read on.**
- Read model examples of how spiritual practices can be incorporated on a regular basis, **read on.**

Chapter 10

Practices that Forge Identity in Christ

Up until now, we've talked about the battles our children are facing and the example Jesus gave through His own life. But knowing the problem and the answer are still not the same as really knowing how to live it out every day.

Identity in Christ is not formed by one sermon, one prayer, or one emotional moment. It is formed through repeated encounters with God in safe, intentional spaces. It is shaped through relationships, habits, and most importantly, "practices" that slowly teach a child, "This is who you are. This is who God is. And this is how you stay connected to Him."

That is why this part of the book focuses on practices. Not rituals for the sake of routine, and not religious activities meant to impress, but simple, life-giving ways that Jesus Himself lived. These practices will, hopefully, create room for the Holy Spirit to speak, heal, correct, and anchor a child's heart in truth. But these aren't just for children; they are also meant for parents, grandparents, teachers, mentors, and spiritual leaders who walk closely with a child and want to help shape their identity in Christ, not just hope it happens on its own (nothing does).

In each practice, you will see the same pattern repeated, so you can clearly understand how to use it. You will first see a "real-life example," because children learn through relationships and experience. Then you will see a biblical example, showing how God has always worked this way. You will see how this practice specifically benefits Generation Alpha, what signs to look for that a child is ready for it, the Scriptures that strengthen to support it, and finally, simple steps for how to apply it in everyday life.

Again, it's important to mention that these are not formulas that guarantee perfect outcomes, but they are pathways that will hopefully create consistent spiritual covering. They will help children not only learn about God, but also learn how to walk with Him. And as they will walk with Him, their identity will begin to settle, not in what they feel, what they fear, or what the world tells them, but in who they are in Christ.

Practice 1: Epistle Writing (Spiritual Letter Writing)

One of the simplest and most powerful ways to shape a child's identity in Christ is through written words. And letters not only slow life down, they also allow truth, encouragement, correction, and love to be received without interruption or defensiveness. In Scripture, God repeatedly used letters to form, guide, and strengthen His people. Epistle writing follows this same pattern by creating a safe space where a child can be seen, affirmed, and spiritually guided over time.

Real-Life Example

Tiffany was beginning to show signs of rebellion against the corrections her mother would give her about her tone of voice, attitude, and disobedience. She would respond by rolling her eyes, sucking her teeth, and speaking rudely to her teachers in school.

Tiffany had a grandmother who lived in another state. Though she loved the warmth of her grandmother's love, her heart had begun to grow distant from her. She wasn't really sure what she liked about her grandmother, but she knew that her grandmother was unique and a strong role model in her life. She also loved the beautiful perfume her grandmother would wear.

After coming home from school one day, Tiffany noticed a letter in the mail with a pink envelope. She was surprised that an envelope was in the mail just for her. After opening it, she noticed beautiful stationery and a handwritten letter. It was her grandmother.

It started out, Dear Tiffany, oh how I miss you ...

The letter detailed what her grandmother had been up to lately and shared a story about when she was growing up and how things were tough for her. Her grandmother explained that she had not liked her own mother very much when she was young, but after looking back, she could see the love her mother had always had for her.

Her grandmother also included a ten-dollar bill, and Tiffany could not have been happier.

Tiffany looked forward to these letters as they came on a monthly basis throughout her youth and teen years. They became an anchor to who she grew up to be. The subtle instructions from her grandmother, and even her candidness, created a space for her to ponder what she was being taught about God and layered her faith in Him.

Biblical Example

My dear son Timothy in the faith,

Night and day I pray constantly for you, building a memorial for you with my prayers. I know that you have wept for me, your spiritual father, and your tears are dear to me. I can't wait to see you again! I'm filled with joy as I think of your strong faith that was passed down through your family line. It began with your grandmother Lois, who passed it on to your dear mother, Eunice. And it's clear that you too are following in the footsteps of their godly example.

I'm writing to encourage you to fan into a flame and rekindle the fire of the spiritual gift God imparted to you when I laid my hands upon you. For God will never give you the spirit of fear, but the Holy Spirit who gives you mighty power, love, and self-control. So never be ashamed of the testimony of our Lord, nor be embarrassed over my imprisonment, but overcome every evil by the revelation of the power of God. — 2 Timothy 1:1–8, TPT

Perhaps you've heard that Phygelus, Hermogenes, and all the believers of Asia have deserted me because of my imprisonment. Nevertheless, so many times Onesiphorus was like a breath of fresh air to me and never seemed to be ashamed of my chains.

May our Lord Jesus bestow compassion and mercy upon him and his household. For when he arrived in Rome, he searched and searched for me until he found out where I was being held, so that he could minister to me, just like he did so wonderfully as I rested in his house while in Ephesus, as you well know. May Jesus, our Master, give him abundant mercy in the day he stands before Him. — 2 Timothy 1:15–18, TPT

Epistle writing is one of the most effective tools that I have used in the past. I personally used it with my own children, using a notebook that went back and forth between my son writing to me about anything he may have been experiencing, and me or his dad responding to him.

This practice has been such an effective tool in my son's spiritual development. I would scaffold thoughts and concepts in great detail according to spiritual truths, while he would express himself with questions, confusion, or misconceptions.

Because of this practice, during his younger years, the lines of communication remained open even as spiritual matters grew more complex.

Practices are not guarantees of perfect spiritual journeys, but they are gateways that help provide answers when the journey gets bumpy. We used a journal notebook that captured much of our communication, but for relatives or spiritual leaders who live far away from the child they love, stationery can also be used.

Through Paul's letters, we can hear the passion and care he had for his spiritual son, Timothy. Paul's writings became transformational because words on paper allowed his authority to speak into Timothy's life.

Paul not only shared his desire to see Timothy grow in his faith, but in the latter part of his letter, he also showed his own vulnerability and human need. This, in itself, develops trust and authenticity.

Many times, Paul was absent, either ministering far away or even imprisoned. Yet this way of communicating created a lasting bond that was just as effective as being face to face.

Parents, grandparents, and spiritual leaders can be intentional, whether they are near or far, in providing apprenticeship letters that scaffold spiritual journeys and express the desires they have for the special youth in their lives to flourish.

Where Generation Alpha Is with Writing

Today's children are the first generation to grow up fully immersed in constant connectivity and advanced technology. Many of them have access to personal tablets and phones from a very young age, which has shaped how they communicate. They are used to short messages, quick visuals, and instant responses. Because of this, many struggle with sustained attention, long-form reading, and traditional writing.

Research often suggests that Generation Alpha is less likely to engage deeply with handwritten communication than previous generations, and this shows up in declining literacy levels and difficulty staying focused for extended periods. Writing, for many of them, feels slow and unfamiliar compared to the fast pace of digital interaction.

How Epistle Writing and Spiritual Letters Can Benefit Generation Alpha

Even with this digital shift, the benefits of journaling and letter writing are well-documented in psychological and educational research and apply strongly to Generation Alpha.

Writing helps children process emotions, regulate stress, and make sense of complex feelings. It gives their thoughts a place to land instead of remaining tangled in their minds. It also strengthens memory, improves focus, sharpens critical thinking, and supports problem-solving skills.

Receiving handwritten letters from parents, grandparents, or spiritual leaders adds something especially powerful. A physical letter carries warmth, intention, and personal presence in a way that texts and screens cannot. It becomes a tangible reminder of love, guidance, and spiritual covering, and it creates a lasting record of encouragement and truth that a child can return to again and again.

Signs a Child May Benefit from Epistle Writing

This practice can be especially helpful when:

- The child finds it hard to connect with others.
- The child is in need of affirmation.
- Distance keeps you from apprenticing them in Christ.
- The child is showing signs of distancing from their faith.
- The child is lacking consistent spiritual leadership.

These are moments when written words can become a bridge, carrying encouragement, correction, and identity-forming truth straight into the heart.

Supporting Scriptures

- 1 & 2 Timothy
- 2 Corinthians 3:2–3
- John 20:31
- Exodus 17:14

Steps to Practicing Epistle Writing with a Child

(This can be done through a shared notebook or through handwritten letters and stationery.)

1. Consider any challenges the child may be facing.
2. Find appropriate stationery or a notebook for writing.
3. Pray and ask God what you can say to this child that would bear fruit, empower them in Christ, and affirm His love for them.
4. Write the letter as you pray before God.
5. Send or give the letter to the child.
6. Create time for reflection and discussion about the contents, and establish a gentle rhythm of writing, especially during seasons of both difficulty and growth.

Practice 2: Communion

While epistle writing helps a child find out who they are through encouragement and support, Communion helps them find out where they belong. Communion is often reduced to a ritual yet it is so much more than that. During Communion there is an assembling together with other believers in the faith. Assembling as the body of Christ is a formation distinct to believers aligning their identity in Christ. It shows them that they aren't following God on their own but are part of a bigger family and a community. More than anything is the vulnerable request Christ made to His people to remember His deep love and great sacrifice for them. Our children experience so much within their spiritual formation when Communion is done in this light. It's where they learn that Christ is not someone we talk about—He is our identity.

Real-Life Example

As they sat together for a time of Communion with siblings and cousins, Aunt Lolo gently set the tone. She said, "This is a space where we are in unity. No one is allowed to shame anyone for how they feel. Instead, we must comfort, forgive, and apologize if we have hurt someone. This is what true Communion is, guys. Is there anyone in this group who has been struggling in any way?"

The room grew silent, but Aunt Lolo waited.

Finally, Juan mumbled that he was struggling. Aunt Lolo leaned in and asked, "What is it, Juan?"

He said, "I just feel like cousin Reg does not include me, and I'm beginning to hate coming here. Him and Tim are always playing games, and I try to jump in, but they keep me out."

Reg and Tim looked at Juan quietly. Aunt Lolo then asked, "What can we do, guys? We will not have Communion until we are in unity."

Tim spoke up. "I didn't know you felt that way. It's just that you are so much younger than us, and sometimes you can't play as fast as we can ... but we love you."

Reg added, "I have to admit, I'm more used to playing with Tim, but I'll do better and try to include you more. I'm sorry. Would you forgive me?"

Some of the other children also resolved conflicts. When the atmosphere was clear and hearts were restored, Aunt Lolo read the Scripture about Communion, and they shared the bread and the wine, representing the body and blood of Christ. Memories of practices like these will never be forgotten in the hearts and minds of these children, and they will always associate forgiving others with Communion and ultimately with Christ as their identity.

Biblical Example

"And he took bread, and when he had given thanks, he broke it and gave it to them, saying, 'This is my body, which is given for you. Do this in remembrance of me.' And likewise, the cup after they had eaten, saying, 'This cup is the new covenant in my blood, which is poured out for you.'" (Luke 22:19–21)

Where Generation Alpha is Today

Generation Alpha is growing up in a fast, digital world where they are constantly connected, yet many still feel deeply lonely. Even with group chats, social media, and online games, they are craving something screens cannot give them: real, face-to-face connection, a sense of belonging, and safe spaces where they are seen, heard, and valued. Their hearts long for community that is not performative, but personal.

Communion meets this need in a powerful way. It brings them into a shared, sacred moment that reminds them they are part of something bigger than themselves, the family of God. It connects their natural desire to care about others, stand for what is right, and make a difference in the world with a living faith they can experience, not just talk about. Through reflection, forgiveness, and unity, Communion helps turn belief into practice, and spectators into participants in the life of Christ and His body.

How Generation Alpha can Benefit from Communion

Communion offers something deeply grounding and needed. Even though Alpha kids are constantly connected online, many still feel lonely, overwhelmed, and emotionally stretched. They long for real, in-person connection that feels safe and meaningful. Communion creates that kind of space. It gathers them physically with others, reminds them they belong to the family of God, and places them in a rhythm of unity, love, and shared faith. Being surrounded by peers and trusted adults in a sacred moment helps build lasting relationships and strengthens both emotional health and spiritual roots.

Communion also teaches them to slow down and look inward. It invites them to examine their hearts, reflect on their choices, seek forgiveness, and realign themselves with God's truth. What might otherwise feel like distant or abstract Bible teachings become real and personal in these moments.

As they take part, they are no longer just hearing about faith, they are practicing it. Over time, this shapes them into active disciples who can recognize God's work in their own lives and in the community around them, carrying a deep sense of belonging, purpose, and spiritual identity into their future.

Supporting Scriptures

Luke 22:19-20

1 Corinthians 11:27-29

Revelations 3:20

John 6:53-58

Signs to Engage This Practice with Youth

Communion is a practice that becomes especially important when certain signs appear in a child's life. Look for these signals:

- The child feels isolated or lacks a sense of community.
- They struggle to understand or grasp the meaning of salvation.
- They have a strong need to belong, to be seen, accepted, and included.

When these signs are present, Communion can provide a powerful space to address both spiritual and emotional needs, helping the child feel connected to God and others in a tangible way.

Steps for Practicing Communion with Youth

Communion is more than a ritual—it's a chance to build unity, trust, and spiritual identity. Here's a step-by-step way to guide children through it:

1. Begin by modeling vulnerability. Share with the child a sin or burden that carries some level of shame in your own life.
2. Create a safe space where each child can confess their own struggles, if and when they feel ready.
3. Establish clear boundaries: no one should attack, mock, or belittle what someone else shares.
4. Ask everyone to agree to respect these boundaries, ensuring that each child feels safe and accepted.
5. Address and resolve any offenses, fostering mutual love and reconciliation among the group.
6. Include moments of shared love and connection, reinforcing the idea of common union.
7. Teach how this unity reflects our oneness with Christ and His promises in Scripture.

8. Explain how Christ's sacrifice—His blameless suffering on the cross—releases us from the consequences of sin when we accept it personally.
9. Lead the children in partaking of the bread and drink, reading Scripture as they do so.
10. Follow Communion with an intentional activity that encourages unity—play a group game, share a meal, or work on a simple task together—modeling love and cooperation in a practical way.

By following these steps, Communion becomes more than a symbolic act; it transforms into a lived experience of faith, belonging, and identity in Christ. It is a practice that lasts a lifetime and is applicable in the many phases of life

Practice 3: Sabbatical Rest

In our fast-paced world, many children tie their worth to achievements, grades, or winning in sports and games. Sabbatical rest is a practice designed to give them a space to pause, reflect, and experience God's unconditional love. It's a time to step away from performance, distractions, and the pressures of success to simply rest in the presence of God and the assurance of their identity in Him.

Real-Life Example

Steve was an honor roll student whose schedule was packed with sports, violin, and video games. Lately, he had just lost a football game and got a C on his math test. His identity felt tied to winning and performing well—he wanted his father to be proud and feared losing that love. That Sunday morning, Steve felt crushed by these failures and unsure of who he was beyond his accomplishments.

A friend invited him to a family "rest day." On this day, nothing was required except walking, playing, and simply admiring God's creation. No cleaning, no chores, no distractions—just space to reflect on God's love and nurture his own love for Him and His world. After spending the day this way, Steve realized something powerful: the best love is unconditional—it doesn't depend on grades, trophies, or winning games. He found his worth in a new way and that was in Christ. It wasn't about cleaning his room or winning a game. Instead, it was in the steadfast love of God where he never needed to produce something to earn love and acceptance.

Biblical Example

At that time Jesus went through the grainfields on the Sabbath. His disciples were hungry and began to pick some heads of grain and eat them. [2] When the Pharisees saw this, they said to him, "Look! Your disciples are doing what is unlawful on the Sabbath."

[3] He answered, "Haven't you read what David did when he and his companions were hungry? [4] He entered the house of God, and he and his companions ate the consecrated bread—which was not lawful for them to do, but only for the priests. [5] Or haven't you read in the Law that the priests on Sabbath duty in the temple desecrate the Sabbath and yet are innocent? [6] I tell you that something greater than the temple is here. [7] If you had known what these words mean, 'I desire mercy, not sacrifice,'[a] you would not have condemned the innocent. [8] For the Son of Man is Lord of the Sabbath." (Matthew 12:1-8)

Cultural Example: Shabbat Walks

On crisp Saturday mornings in Brooklyn, New York, or along the winding streets of Teaneck, New Jersey, groups of Jewish families move quietly through the city, like pearls threading along a string. Fathers in dark coats and wide-brimmed hats walk beside their sons, whose soft curls, called *payot*, bounce gently with each step. Mothers push strollers with babies wrapped in warm blankets, while older daughters, modestly dressed in skirts that sway with their movement, walk arm-in-arm with grandmothers who have been keeping this tradition for decades. There is no chatter about errands, no phones buzzing in pockets. Just the soft crunch of gravel under polished shoes and the gentle hum of anticipation. The city keeps going, but for these families, time seems to bend. Saturday is not a day for striving or rushing; it is a day to return—to themselves, to their souls, and to the One who calls them "people of rest."

This scene is not just nostalgia wrapped in wool coats or the smell of fresh challah. Research from Jewish educational institutions and mental health journals shows that these Shabbat walks—slow, shared, and intentional—help anchor young people in their identities. For teens caught between TikTok trends, school pressure, and college worries, the steady rhythm of walking with family while reflecting on Scripture offers a kind of inner calm that the rest of life rarely allows. It teaches them to see their bodies as holy rather than shameful, and their identity as whole rather than broken. Unlike traditions that fade into history, this one lives in the streets, in the quiet moments between questions and answers, where boys twirl their curls absentmindedly, girls hold their prayer books carefully, and the soul remembers it was made for more than noise and confusion.

In Brooklyn, where my Haitian parents settled after immigrating, I often watched these families with a sense of awe. Boys walked beside fathers in black suits and high hats, girls held their mothers' or grandmothers' hands, and everyone moved quietly, focused on the day, without phones or errands interrupting. Time slowed, and Saturday became not a day for achievement or obligation but a day for rest—for returning to themselves, to their families, and to God.

As an inner-city public-school teacher and Sunday school youth teacher, this made me pause. These families had continued this practice for generations, from children as young as eight to elders in their eighties. Meanwhile, the youth I worked with at church often rushed out as soon as the service ended, and the students I taught were struggling with anxiety, hyper sexualization, and questions about who they were. Watching these families, I wondered if some of these Eastern biblical practices could teach the Western world something valuable.

Research backs this up. These Shabbat walks—slow, intentional, and shared—help young people build a strong sense of who they are. Walking with family, reflecting on Scripture, and taking time to pause brings calm, self-respect, and a sense of wholeness. Their bodies are honored, their identities are affirmed, and their souls remember they are made for more than confusion, shame, and the endless noise of life.

Where Generation Alpha Is with Rest

Research on how Generation Alpha experiences rest and leisure away from screens, competitive sports, or identity-forming productivity is still in its early stages, largely because this group is mostly very young. Emerging trends, however, show that parents and educators are becoming increasingly aware of the importance of "unplugged" time to support children's mental health and cognitive development. This often looks like simple outdoor play, creative arts, or quiet reading, though these activities are constantly competing with highly engaging digital alternatives. One of the challenges in studying this kind of leisure is that technology and structured activities are so deeply woven into modern childhood that purely tech-free, demand-free play rarely happens naturally. For many Alpha children, unplugged time is a deliberate, parent-led choice rather than something they fall into on their own.

How Sabbatical Rest Can Benefit Generation Alpha

The long-term benefits for Generation Alpha in adopting an identity rooted in true rest and sabbatical practices are profound. Such practices provide an essential counterbalance to the "hustle culture" that this generation is already inheriting. When rest is embraced as a valid, intentional pursuit—not just a break from work—it fosters creativity, resilience, and emotional intelligence. Nathan T. Stucky, a theologian who writes on Sabbath and spiritual formation, argues that practicing Sabbath challenges the modern belief that human worth is tied to productivity. Instead, Sabbath invites people to rest in an identity grounded in God's grace rather than in what they produce.[17]

For Alpha children, this perspective encourages them to find intrinsic value beyond grades, achievements, or accomplishments. As Stucky emphasizes, through rest, "We discover that we are more than the sum of our tasks." Developing an identity that is comfortable with rest and sabbatical periods can help young people build a more balanced, sustainable life, free from constant performance anxiety. It reminds them, and the adults guiding them, that "our value is not in what we do, but who we are as God's beloved."

Signs to Engage This Practice with Youth

1. **Chronic stress or anxiety** – The child seems overwhelmed by school, extracurriculars, or social pressures and shows signs of mental fatigue.
2. **Over-identifying with achievements** – Their sense of self-worth is tied to grades, awards, sports wins, or other accomplishments.

[17] Nathan T. Stucky, Wrestling with Rest: Inviting Youth to Discover the Gift of Sabbath (Grand Rapids, MI: Eerdmans, 2019).

3. **Difficulty focusing or burnout** – They show fatigue, irritability, or lack of motivation despite high effort.
4. **Constant busyness** – Their schedule is packed, leaving little time for reflection, play, or quiet activities.
5. **Struggles with identity** – They question who they are beyond performance or peer approval.
6. **Emotional volatility** – Frequent frustration, impatience, or sadness that seems disproportionate to the situation.
7. **Disconnection from God or self** – Spiritual practices feel rushed or absent, and they seem unaware of their inner life or feelings.
8. **Resistance to rest or unstructured time** – They complain about boredom, insist on constant activity, or feel anxious when asked to pause.

Supporting Scriptures

- Luke 6:5
- Matthew 12:1-8
- Hebrews 4:9

Steps for Practicing Sabbath Rest with Youth

1. Select a day for the child to abandon activities that require production including chores.
2. Agree that this day will be spent on nothing else but speaking about God, doing things in remembrance of God, and building an identity that connects to just being unconditionally loved and forgiven by Him.
3. Include a day out in nature and point out God's creation and discuss why He placed some things on Earth for the child.

4. Create an art or craft that points back to God. This can include art, dance, song, music, or any form of godly expression.
5. Close the day with reflection. Have them share their favorite part.
6. Close the day in prayer.

Practice 4: Repentance

Repentance is one of the most powerful practices for building a child's identity in Christ because it teaches them how to recognize their own faults, release resentment, and experience God's grace firsthand. Just as each previous practice (epistle writing, Communion, and sabbatical rest) anchors identity through action, repentance anchors the heart by cultivating humility, honesty, and reconciliation.

Real-Life Example

Robert carried a deep hatred for his father, who had left him and his mother without ever reaching out. He longed to know his father but his anger was stronger than his desire. At school, Robert hid behind a tough exterior, cursing teachers or storming out when anything triggered him.

One day, his uncle, Bernard, took him for a haircut. On the drive home, Bernard shared his own story of growing up without a father, revealing how his own anger had caused him deep trouble until he asked God to forgive him. Hearing his uncle's vulnerable confession, Robert unexpectedly broke down, crying for what felt like an eternity. Bernard placed a steady hand on his shoulder and said, "I know your father hurt you, but you must forgive him. Son, you are not fatherless. I am here for you, and you have a Father in heaven who wants to heal you if you will let Him."

This moment of shared vulnerability allowed Robert to begin letting go of anger and opening his heart to God's healing, showing how repentance can restore identity and relational connection. Uncle Bernard modeled how Robert was to speak to adults like his teacher, and Robert's forgiveness toward his father was a well that nourished the desert spaces in his heart.

Biblical Example

The story of the prodigal son perfectly illustrates repentance and reconciliation:

"When he came to his senses, he said, 'How many of my father's hired servants have food to spare, and here I am starving to death! I will set out and go back to my father and say to him: Father, I have sinned against heaven and against you. I am no longer worthy to be called your son; make me like one of your hired servants.' So he got up and went to his father. But while he was still a long way off, his father saw him and was filled with compassion for him; he ran to his son, threw his arms around him, and kissed him. The son said to him, 'Father, I have sinned against heaven and against you. I am no longer worthy to be called your son.'" —Luke 15:17-21

Just like Robert, the prodigal son faced the weight of shame, anger, and regret, but by choosing to turn back, through repentance, he was restored to relationship and security in his father's love.

Where Generation Apha Is When It Comes to Repentance

Generation Alpha's relationship with biblical repentance is complicated. They're growing up in a world that is highly connected, digital, and socially conscious, where personal authenticity and moral relativism often take center stage over traditional, absolute truths. Many in this generation are being raised in environments where adherence to traditional religious institutions is declining, and some studies suggest they may struggle with, or even reject, the biblical definition of "sin" that calls for repentance. Instead, they often focus on tangible actions: standing against injustice, helping those in need, and accepting people for who they are. For many Alphas, moral decisions are guided more by real-world impact than abstract theological concepts.

That said, this doesn't mean they are closed off to spirituality or to the principles behind repentance, such as personal accountability or striving for a better life. Generation Alpha values authenticity, fairness, and transparency—even in the institutions they engage with, including churches. Ministry leaders observe that when young people see faith actively transforming lives, they respond. The idea of repentance—a genuine change of heart and turning from wrongdoing—resonates most when it is tied to hope, purpose, and real-life outcomes, like service, reconciliation, and restorative justice. Many Alphas are spiritually curious, believe in a higher power, and recognize the importance of faith in their lives. They are open to exploring spiritual concepts, especially when these ideas help them make sense of the complex world around them in practical, meaningful ways.

How Repentance Can Benefit Generation Alpha

Generation Alpha, born from the early 2010s through 2025, is growing up in a time defined by rapid technological change, constant digital connectivity, and social upheaval. Biblical repentance, which involves a deep change of heart that leads to new actions and a restored relationship with God, offers critical benefits for this generation. Right now, practicing repentance can help young Alphas navigate the pressures of a digital world, including the temptations of compulsive scrolling, online conflicts, or even cyberbullying. By reflecting on their actions, taking responsibility, and seeking to correct their mistakes, they can develop emotional resilience, self-control, empathy, and patience. Learning to recognize wrongdoing and intentionally choose a new path gives them a moral compass in a world where ethical boundaries are often blurred.

Looking ahead, integrating repentance into their spiritual lives equips Alpha children with skills that will serve them well into adulthood. The ability to admit fault, seek forgiveness, and change direction is essential for personal growth, ethical decision-making, and leadership. As they encounter complex issues in technology, social systems, and environmental stewardship, this practice encourages them to prioritize communal well-being and ethical responsibility over purely individual goals. In the long term, a foundation in repentance fosters strong, character-driven adults who can cultivate meaningful relationships and build compassionate, values-driven communities—grounded not in fleeting trends, but in enduring principles.

Signs to Engage Practice with Youth (Repentance)

- The child reacts with anger, bitterness, or unresolved resentment toward family, friends, or authority figures.
- They hold grudges or struggle to forgive others, showing difficulty letting go of past hurts.
- They frequently make the same mistakes or display repeated harmful behaviors without acknowledging consequences.
- The child expresses guilt, shame, or self-condemnation but struggles to take constructive action.
- They avoid talking about or reflecting on mistakes, whether in private or in safe spaces.
- Distance or avoidance in relationships suggests they are struggling with accountability or relational repair.
- Signs of moral confusion or uncertainty about right and wrong, especially in socially complex or digital situations.

- The child shows openness or curiosity when seeing examples of honesty, vulnerability, or reconciliation in others.

Supporting Scriptures

- 2 Corinthians 7:10
- Luke 15:7
- Matthew 3:8
- Luke 5:32
- Acts 3:19

Steps for Practicing Repentance with Youth

1. Discuss the wrongdoing.
2. Share a time when you did wrong.
3. Show supporting Scriptures.
4. Allow the child to share their thoughts.
5. Ask if they are ready to repent.
6. If so, lead them into prayer but allow them to pray with you, verbalizing where they are and their statement of repentance.
7. Affirm them regularly as you spend time with them.

Practice 5: Forgiveness

Forgiveness is one of the most powerful practices for shaping a child's identity in Christ. It goes beyond just saying "I'm sorry" or letting someone off the hook—it teaches them how to release bitterness, reconcile relationships, and reflect God's love in their daily lives. In a world where children are constantly navigating conflict, injustice, and social pressures, learning to forgive helps them develop empathy, emotional resilience, and a deeper understanding of God's grace. This practice shows young people that their identity is not defined by the wrongs done to them, but by the way they choose to respond—and that choosing forgiveness can anchor their hearts and minds in Christ, even in the midst of hurt.

Real Life Example

A lump lived in Jeronimo's throat. How could his own friends have jumped him and left him in such pain? The authorities had been called after he was found beaten, with punch wounds that went deeper than the knot on his forehead. The boys who did this to him were expelled from school and placed in a juvenile center. But that punishment wasn't enough to heal Jeronimo. He kept asking himself: Why couldn't I fight back? Why were they able to overtake me?

The words from a church sermon echoed in his mind: "Sometimes the deepest scars we carry are the anger we hold from being unjustly wronged." For over three years, Jeronimo walked with his head down, carrying that lump in his throat, replaying the pain over and over.

Eventually, he began to reflect on how God had forgiven the very people who put Him on the cross. Slowly, Jeronimo softened. After a week of meditating on the agony Jesus endured, he began to connect with God and started the difficult but freeing process of forgiving those who had wronged him.

Biblical Example

Then Joseph said to them, "Don't be afraid. Can I do what only God can do? You meant to hurt me, but God turned your evil into good to save the lives of many people, which is being done. So don't be afraid. I will take care of you and your children." So, Joseph comforted his brothers and spoke kind words to them.

Joseph continued to live in Egypt with all his father's family. He died when he was one hundred ten years old.

Where Generation Alpha Is When It Comes to Forgiveness

Many young people today are growing up in a world where conversations about justice, accountability, and fairness are common. Yet the practice of forgiveness, both giving it and receiving it, often feels more complicated. Research suggests that even among practicing Christians there can be a disconnect between the two. In a 2019 Barna Group study, 76 percent of practicing Christians said they believe they have offered unconditional forgiveness to someone who hurt them, yet only 55 percent say they remember someone extending that same kind of forgiveness to them. This gap suggests that while many believe they are forgiving others, fewer recall experiencing forgiveness themselves, pointing to a difference between how forgiveness is perceived and how it is actually experienced.

How Generation Alpha Can Benefit Now from Forgiveness

Right now, many children and teens in Generation Alpha are growing up in a world of constant comparison, online conflict, cancel culture, and emotional overwhelm. Offenses don't just happen face-to-face anymore, they live on screens, in group chats, in comments, and in public memory. Learning forgiveness gives them an emotional and spiritual way to release resentment before it hardens into identity. It teaches them that what happened to them does not have to define them, and that their worth is not shaped by rejection, betrayal, or humiliation. Forgiveness also helps regulate anger, reduce anxiety, and restore trust, which are essential for healthy relationships with parents, peers, and authority figures.

Spiritually, forgiveness grounds them in the heart of the gospel. When they learn that they are deeply forgiven by God, they become less driven by shame and more open to repentance, healing, and growth. This builds humility, empathy, and emotional maturity early on, rather than letting bitterness quietly shape their personality and worldview.

How Forgiveness Can Benefit Generation Alpha in the Future

As this generation grows into adulthood, leadership, marriage, parenting, and ministry will all require the ability to forgive deeply and consistently. Unforgiveness fractures communities, families, churches, and even entire movements. A generation trained in forgiveness will be far more capable of reconciliation, conflict resolution, and restorative justice. Instead of becoming hardened, defensive, or emotionally closed, they can become adults who know how to confront wrong, seek healing, and rebuild trust.

On an identity level, forgiveness anchors them in who they are in Christ rather than in what was done to them. It frees them from carrying unresolved pain into their future roles and relationships. Learning to forgive does not erase justice or truth, but it releases the soul from being imprisoned by the past. In this way, forgiveness becomes not just a moral act, but a lifelong spiritual discipline that protects their hearts, preserves unity, and allows them to walk in emotional and spiritual freedom.

Signs to Engage Forgiveness as a Practice with Youth

1. They hold on to grudges easily.
2. They do not understand that Christ's theme was all about forgiveness.

Supporting Scriptures

- Ephesians 4:32
- Colossians 3:13
- Isaiah 1:18
- Psalm 51:7

Steps to Engage Forgiveness as a Practice with Youth

1. Have them vulnerably share the offense verbally or in writing.
2. Let them know you hear their pain.
3. Share a time where you experienced injustice.
4. Share the injustice endured by Christ.
5. Show in Scripture how He forgave our offense as sinners.
6. Work regularly with the youth in prayer and Bible study until they are able to fully release the offense and forgive.

Practice 6: Text in Context

In a world where information comes in fast, fragmented pieces, children are constantly forming beliefs based on short clips, isolated quotes, and viral opinions. When it comes to Scripture, this can be especially dangerous. "Text in Context" teaches young people that God's Word is not meant to be consumed in soundbites but understood as a unified story. This practice trains them to slow down, read carefully, and learn how to interpret what God is saying by looking at the whole picture, not just a single verse.

Cultural literacy tools like the following support youth in gaining context as they create vivid understanding of the Bible:

Timelines that provide context with where the child is as it relates to present and historical Scripture

Maps that provide geographical locations with where the child is as it relates to Scripture

Cultural references that discuss traditions, practices of Biblical periods

Concordance that allows for Scripture-based studies

Greek and Hebrew dictionaries that add meaning to Bible studies

Real Life Example

Eleven-year-old Jeremy read many stories from the Bible yet at some point the stories did not land in a way that was clear or organized. They seemed like random stories that could stand alone with no connections to other parts of the Bible. Jeremy's grandmother noticed this as Jeremy seemed to grow bored with the stories. After talking to one of the church leaders for suggestions on this, Jeremy's grandmother decided to provide small frameworks that would add context to the Bible for Jeremy. She started out by sharing and explaining the various genres of the Bible along with their meaning. Some of the genres included Laws, History, Poetry, Wisdom Literature, Prophecy, Gospels, and Epistles (Letters). This provided Jeremy with an organized understanding of the Bible. In the following year, Jeremy's grandmother spent time explaining timeframes of the Bible such as B.C (before Christ) and A. D (Anno Domino- After Christ). Next, she added a Bible timeline from the Old Testament and the New Testament that Jeremy could reference when bible reading took place so that Jeremy could refer to it. Jeremy's grandmother even added the year Jeremy was born within the timeline in order for Jeremy to see his life in light of the Bible timeline. During Bible studies where Jeremy required more depth, Jeremy's grandmother introduced him to a concordance in order to search other scriptures related to the topic while also gaining the Greek and Hebrew meaning of words. By the time Jeremy turned 17, he was familiar with timelines, concordance, maps, Bible cultural literacy and many tools that enhanced his understanding on the Word of God. These tools provided Jeremy with personal ownership in his ability to know and understand God's Word for himself. Tools that provide text in context helped Jeremy to be anchored in his faith where few distractions could pull him away from a lasting faith.

Biblical Example

They received the message with great eagerness and examined the Scriptures every day to see if what Paul said was true. As a result, many of them believed, as did also several prominent Greek women and many Greek men. (Acts 17:10-12)

Where Generation Alpha Is Now as It Relates to Literacy

Generation Alpha is the first generation to grow up fully immersed in digital life from infancy. As a result, their relationship with reading looks very different from previous generations. Recent data shows that only about 30 percent of Generation Alpha fourth graders were reading at a proficient level in 2024, reflecting a noticeable decline in foundational reading skills. This trend is often linked to the heavy presence of screens in daily life, including educational devices that also double as sources of constant distraction through games, apps, and short-form video content.

Because so much of their information comes through quick, visually-driven platforms like YouTube and TikTok, many Alpha children are becoming accustomed to scanning rather than deeply reading. This affects their ability to engage in what researchers call "deep reading," the kind of focused, sustained attention needed to understand complex ideas, follow arguments, recognize themes, and interpret figurative language. While many can process surface-level information quickly, they often struggle with analyzing meaning, evaluating context, and drawing thoughtful conclusions from longer texts. Educators are now working to reintroduce habits that strengthen attention, comprehension, and critical thinking alongside the use of technology.

How "Text in Context" Can Benefit Generation Alpha

Biblical literacy can serve as a stabilizing anchor for Generation Alpha in a world overflowing with information, opinions, and competing worldviews. Learning to read Scripture thoughtfully gives them a moral and spiritual framework that helps them make sense of life, truth, and identity. As they grow, this practice develops critical thinking, historical awareness, and an understanding of the values that have shaped both faith and culture. Instead of being shaped primarily by trends and algorithms, they learn to evaluate ideas through the lens of God's Word.

Teaching children to compare Scripture with Scripture also trains them to resist taking verses out of context or forming beliefs based on isolated passages. This habit encourages patience, careful study, and a respect for the unity of the Bible's message. For a generation used to consuming decontextualized content, learning to read the Bible as a connected, coherent story helps build a deeper, more resilient faith. It grounds them in truth that is not easily swayed by partial interpretations, emotional reactions, or online soundbites, and helps them grow into believers who understand not just what the Bible says, but what it truly means.

Signs to Engage Text-in-Context as a Practice with Youth

- The child quotes Bible verses but seems confused about what they really mean or applies them in ways that don't fit the situation.
- They ask honest questions about God, faith, or difficult passages and feel unsettled by contradictions they think they see in Scripture.
- They are heavily influenced by social media theology, short clips, or trending opinions about God, and need help learning how to discern truth.
- They struggle with focus when reading the Bible and tend to jump from verse to verse without understanding the larger story.

- They show a growing desire to know *why* they believe what they believe, not just *what* they believe.
- They are beginning to form their own identity and worldview and need a solid biblical framework to interpret life, suffering, and purpose.

Supporting Scriptures

- 2 Timothy 2:15
- 2Timothy 3:16-17
- Hebrews 4:12
- Acts 8:30-31
- 1 Peter 3:15
- Acts 17:11

Steps to Engage Text-in-Context as a Practice with Youth

1. Take a Scripture reference.
2. Ask them to apply the Lectio Devina method (a reflective practice of slowly reading Scripture, meditating on its meaning, praying about it, and listening for how God may be speaking through the passage).
3. Discuss all parts with them.
4. Select other parts in Scripture that supports this portion of Scripture.

Chapter 11

Practices that Transform Emotional Struggles into Spiritual Strength

Generation Alpha is growing up in a world filled with constant noise, pressure, and digital stimulation, leaving many young people struggling to manage their thoughts, emotions, and sense of identity. Scripture offers a different path by inviting believers into simple spiritual practices that help steady the mind and anchor the heart in God's truth. These practices are not complicated techniques but rhythms that train children and youth to slow down, reflect on God's Word, and develop a deeper awareness of His presence in their daily lives. When practiced consistently, they can help build emotional resilience, spiritual clarity, and a stronger sense of identity in Christ.

Practice 1: Biblical Meditation

Biblical meditation is not about emptying the mind, but about learning how to anchor it. In a world where Generation Alpha is constantly flooded with images, messages, pressure, and stimulation, their minds rarely rest. Thoughts race, emotions spiral, and identity is often shaped by what they see and hear the most. Scripture invites us into a different rhythm, one where the mind is gently trained to dwell on God's truth, to repeat it, reflect on it, and let it settle deep into the heart. This practice builds mental wellness by teaching children and youth how to pause, focus, and allow God's Word to steady their emotions, guide their choices, and remind them who they are when anxiety, temptation, or confusion tries to take over.

Real-Life Example

The thought, "Flee sexual immorality," kept running through Mary's mind. Her friends had been sharing things she knew her parents would not approve of, and more importantly, things she knew God was against. After an inappropriate encounter with a boy on the school bus, her heart began to race. *Flee sexual immorality.* The words echoed again and again.

Her phone rang. It was him. She had a crush on him, but never in a million years did she expect things to move so quickly. At first, she felt special that he even noticed her, but now the situation was becoming something she had never imagined or expected. Should she let him have his way? Was this what it meant to be liked by someone? *Flee sexual immorality* kept playing in her head, and the memory of what had happened left her shaken and confused.

Finally, she surrendered to that inner urging. She chose to flee. She ignored his call and, in tears, reached out to her mother. She confessed everything that was happening and asked her to help her navigate the pressure she was feeling from her peers and the boy on the bus.

Biblical Examples

"Blessed is the one whose delight is in the Lord, and who meditates on his law day and night. That person, or child, is like a tree planted by streams of water, which yields its fruit in season and whose leaf does not wither—whatever they do prospers." (Psalm 1)

If I simply say the word *meditation* in my classroom, my students immediately sit cross-legged with their hands resting on their laps, reflecting the modern, cultural image of meditation. Very few of them are aware of what biblical meditation truly is.

Where Generation Alpha Is with Meditation

Research paints a complex picture of how Generation Alpha engages with cultural and traditional forms of meditation. The sustained focus these practices require often clashes with their technology-driven environment. As digital natives immersed in fast, interactive media, Alpha children typically access religious and spiritual content through platforms like TikTok and YouTube, favoring short, visually engaging clips over slower practices such as reflective reading or quiet contemplation. While they show strong interest in spirituality and values like authenticity and fairness, their engagement with deeper, traditional forms of meditation is less common, partly due to a generational tendency toward skepticism and a desire for immediate, transformational insight rather than information that feels repetitive or abstract.

How Biblical Meditation Can Benefit Generation Alpha

Research suggests that scriptural, Bible-centered meditation could offer Generation Alpha a much-needed anchor in a rapidly changing, technology-saturated world. These practices may help address the rising levels of anxiety and emotional strain already evident in Gen Z and beginning to surface in Gen Alpha by fostering mental clarity, emotional regulation, and the ability to process difficult thoughts, similar to the well-documented benefits of mindfulness. Rooting their strong sense of justice and social awareness in the unchanging truth of God's Word can also provide a stable moral framework and a form of transformational knowledge that goes deeper than the fragmented, surface-level information often encountered online. In this way, biblical meditation can help shape them not as restless wanderers shaped by trends, but as grounded young people becoming architects of a new, faith-centered future.

Supporting Scriptures

- Psalm 1:2
- Joshua 1:8
- Psalm 143:5
- Psalm 119:148
- Philippians 4:8

Before practicing biblical meditation with your child, it helps to understand what meditation truly means in the scriptural sense. Biblical meditation is the act of thinking deeply and carefully about something — questioning, seeking, and turning it over in the mind until it becomes anchored in the heart.

A Step-by-Step Practice for Biblical Meditation with Your Child

1. Evaluate or consider a current way your child has been thinking of something. Consider a brain dump of where they are on a given Scripture, spiritual concept or idea.
2. Select a Scripture that challenges their current thought for growth and shifts into God's way.
3. Model out loud how to take that Scripture apart in your mind in light of your current and natural way of thinking using questions, clarifying Scriptures.
4. Challenge the child to begin shifting their previous thought to the Scripture, as they answer all opposing thoughts that come to mind with the use of the given Scripture and other supporting Scriptures.

5. Discuss what happened through this process.
6. Take 15-30 minutes to think over the focus topic, clarifying it in your mind.
7. Come back together to share lasting thoughts.
8. Agree that meditation will continue throughout the week.
9. Create a board with the written topic for anyone to post notes on added revelation on the topic.
10. Pick a date when you will revisit and add to thoughts that came up that week.

Practice 2: Confession

Before we talk about what confession looks like in real life and in Scripture, it helps to understand why this practice matters so much for our children. Confession is not about shame or punishment; it is about bringing what is hidden into the light so healing can begin. When a child is given a safe space to speak honestly about their thoughts, fears, mistakes, and misunderstandings, they learn that they do not have to carry heavy feelings alone. In the same way God invites us to come to Him openly and be restored, confession teaches the next generation how to release guilt, receive truth, and experience the freedom that comes from being fully known and fully loved.

Real-Life Example

It was unusually quiet in the car as I drove the kids to school that morning. My husband had just spoken to our ten-year-old son about putting things back where they belonged and following directions. Instead of hearing the correction for what it was, our son took it in a very different way. The atmosphere in the car felt heavy as we pulled away.

Finally, I asked, "Hey, are you okay?"

There was no response.

"What's going on?"

Then he quietly said, "Mom ... does Dad hate me?"

I was stunned that my son had interpreted his father's correction as rejection. At the same time, I was so thankful he said it out loud so it could be addressed. As he began to cry, he poured out what he was feeling, and I explained what his father had really meant. I then called my husband and shared how our son was taking the situation. My husband spoke with him, clarified his words, and reassured him of his deep love.

Before the school day even began, my son was able to release that burden and restore a healthy emotional balance with his dad.

Where Generation Alpha Is Now as It Relates to Confession

Generation Alpha, the first generation born entirely in the twenty-first century and shaped by digital life, is growing up in a world with shifting views on traditional spiritual practices such as confession. With declining church involvement and diverse family structures, many children in this generation only encounter faith practices if parents intentionally introduce them. While research shows that Generation Alpha is spiritually curious and deeply values authenticity and fairness, the formal idea of confession, especially in an institutional setting, can feel outdated or rigid to them. They are used to instant communication and immediate feedback, which can make slower, structured spiritual processes feel distant from their everyday experience.

At the same time, the decline of clear, healthy outlets for confession can leave many of these children carrying unspoken guilt, confusion, and emotional weight. Generation Alpha already faces rising levels of anxiety and emotional overload, intensified by social media, comparison, and constant stimulation. Without a safe and trusted space to admit wrongs, express inner struggles, and receive reassurance and forgiveness, these emotions can remain bottled up. While they are encouraged to talk about mental health, many lack a spiritual framework for releasing moral and relational burdens, which can deepen stress and inner conflict.

How Generation Alpha Can Benefit from Confession

Biblical confession offers a powerful path to freedom for Generation Alpha by giving them a safe, structured way to bring hidden struggles into the light and receive grace. It teaches honesty, accountability, and restoration, values this generation already cares deeply about. Confession is not simply admitting wrongdoing, but allowing God to meet them in truth and heal what is broken. It addresses their deep longing to be understood and accepted while guiding them toward genuine transformation rather than quiet shame.

Biblical voices and spiritual leaders have long pointed to the life-changing power of this practice:

- ““To confess your sins to God is not to tell God anything God doesn't already know. Until you confess them, however, they are the abyss between you. When you confess them, they become the Golden Gate Bridge.”[18]
- “Whoever conceals their sins does not prosper, but the one who confesses and renounces them finds mercy” (Proverbs 28:13), showing the direct connection between honesty and healing.
- “We must lay before Him what is in us, not what ought to be within us,” states C.S. Lewis[19]. This quote reminds us that real transformation begins with truthful, vulnerable confession,

[18] Frederick Buechner, *Wishful Thinking: A Theological ABC* (San Francisco: Harper & Row, 1973

[19] C. S. Lewis, *Letters to Malcolm: Chiefly on Prayer* (New York: Harcourt, Brace & World, 1964).

something that resonates deeply with a generation that values authenticity.

Supporting Scriptures

- James 5:16
- Psalm 32:5
- 1 John 1:9

How to Guide Your Child Through Confession

1. Provide the child time with a trusted spiritual leader that the child feels safe with.
2. Provide the child with time of reflection and quiet.
3. Ask them to write or verbally state something that has been bothering them or even something they have done that may displease the Lord.
4. Agree that you will both bring it before the Lord.
5. Share the Scripture on the promise of confession to God.
6. Assure them that you forgive them, and above all, that God forgives them.
7. Close in prayer and rejoice on the gift of forgiveness.

Practice 3: Journaling

Journaling offers a meaningful way for young people to explore their thoughts, feelings, and questions in a safe and reflective space. For Generation Alpha, who is growing up in a fast-paced, digital world where silence and introspection are rare, writing provides a tangible way to slow down, process emotions, and engage with God personally. By putting their experiences, doubts, and joys into words, youth can cultivate a deeper sense of self-awareness, spiritual connection, and emotional clarity, making journaling a powerful practice for building mental wellness in Christ.

Real-Life Example

Jessica was full of wonder about God, but because she had come to know Him through a summer camp—and her faith wasn't nurtured at home by her atheist family—she often struggled to express her thoughts, questions, and feelings. During one of her summer camps, there was an activity where Jessica was asked to write a letter to God. She began, "*Dear God, I am so glad I get to talk to you through writing. I often feel alone in my thoughts, but writing makes it real that my thoughts are important and that you are there to read them. Every time I write, I sense an answer coming into my heart after I finish expressing my thoughts. I guess that's just the Holy Spirit responding to my letter to you. Until next time. Love, Jessica.*"

Biblical Example

My heart overflows with a pleasing theme; I address my verses to the king; my tongue is like the pen of a ready scribe. (Psalm 45:1)

Signs to Engage Journaling as a Practice with Youth

1. The young person struggles to show expression toward God.
2. They enjoy writing.
3. They want to engage with God but do not know how.
4. Talking about God is difficult.
5. Their verbal reasoning is a struggle.
6. They have questions and ideas that are hard to articulate.

Supporting Scriptures

- Habakuk 2:2
- Jeremiah 30:2
- Psalm 45:1

Steps to Engage Journaling as a Practice with Youth

1. Read a few of David's Psalms to the child, emphasizing free expression.
2. Bring attention to the pattern of many of the Psalms, such as acknowledging God, conflict, and resolution from God.
3. Take one of the Psalms and share a dialogue discussion with the child on what David may have been facing at the time.
4. Share how David used writing to release his burdens and even share his joys.
5. Provide a quiet, safe, and relaxing space for the child and allow them to write something to God that has been on their hearts.
6. Have them start the letter with Dear Lord.
7. They may keep the journal private or they may share if they are comfortable.

Practice 4: Reflection

Reflection is a powerful practice that helps young people pause, slow down, and consider both their actions and the world around them through the lens of God's Word. Unlike journaling, which captures thoughts in writing, or meditation, which focuses inwardly on God's presence, reflection encourages a conscious evaluation of life experiences, choices, and relationships in the light of Scripture. For Generation Alpha, who grows up in a fast-paced, constantly connected world, cultivating the habit of reflection provides a much-needed space to process experiences, make thoughtful decisions, and develop self-awareness grounded in faith. This practice not only nurtures spiritual growth but also supports emotional and mental wellness, helping youth align their hearts and minds with God's guidance.

Biblical Example

A reflective Psalm invites a young person to pause and consider what God sees and what that means for their own life. As they read the passage below, they can ask themselves what it reveals about God's justice and how their actions align with His ways.

The Lord is in his holy temple;
the Lord is on his heavenly throne.
He observes everyone on earth; his eyes examine them.
The Lord examines the righteous, but the wicked, those who love violence,
He hates with a passion.
On the wicked he will rain fiery coals and burning sulfur; a scorching wind will be their lot.
For the Lord is righteous, he loves justice; the upright will see his face.

Reflection might then include questions such as: What does this passage teach about the kind of life God values? What attitudes or actions in my own life might need to change?

Where Generation Alpha Is Now as It Relates to Reflection

Generation Alpha is navigating a world filled with constant stimuli, from social media feeds to academic pressures, leaving little room for introspection. Many young people rarely take the time to pause and think critically about their experiences, values, or spiritual growth. While they are naturally curious and capable of deep thought, the habit of structured reflection is not yet widely cultivated, often because fast-paced digital habits prioritize immediate responses over contemplative thinking. Providing intentional opportunities for reflection can help them slow down, connect their experiences to biblical principles, and develop critical thinking skills that integrate both faith and daily life.

Supporting Scriptures

- 2 Corinthians 13:5
- Lamentations 3:40
- Matthew 7:3-5
- Psalm 118:11

Steps to Engage Reflection as a Practice with Youth

1. Preferably go out in nature and find a quiet spot where the beauty of God is evident.
2. Select a situation and couple it with Scripture.
3. Provide fifteen to twenty minutes of time to think over the situation as it relates to the given Scripture.
4. Have each child share their reflection.
5. Affirm them in their reflection.
6. Share your personal reflections.

Chapter 12

Practices that Shift Natural Impulses into Holy Alignment

This chapter explores spiritual practices that help young people shape their understanding of sexuality in ways that reflect the character and design of Christ. In a culture where messages about sex are constant, confusing, and often disconnected from faith, Generation Alpha needs more than rules. They need formation. These practices invite youth to learn how their bodies, desires, relationships, and choices fit within God's larger story of love, dignity, and covenant. When practiced consistently, they help young people develop self-control, respect for others, and a view of sexuality that honors both God and the sacred value of every person made in His image.

Practice 1: Surrender

Surrender, in the context of sexuality, is about learning to submit your desires, impulses, and choices to God's guidance rather than yielding to immediate gratification or cultural pressures. For Generation Alpha, who is growing up in a hypersexualized, digitally-connected world, surrendering is not instinctive. They are encouraged to be independent, assertive, and in control of their lives, which often conflicts with the idea of yielding authority over their desires to God. Yet, surrender offers a pathway to self-control, moral integrity, and a sexuality that aligns with Christ's design—helping young people navigate the challenges of puberty, peer pressure, and exposure to sexualized media with wisdom and grace.

Real-Life Example

Wayne listened as his friends shared all the sexual encounters they had over the weekend. His body surged with desire, wanting to experience the same things, even though he knew it wasn't what he was taught. He understood that these experiences were meant to be reserved for a committed marital relationship, yet every part of him seemed to say, "You need this now." He knew a girl who might give him that opportunity, but a voice inside him warned that pursuing her would be using her. What if someone did that to his sister? He would hate it. Wayne wrestled with these feelings, tossing and turning as they battled within him. These emotions were intense enough to make a twelve-year-old cry, yet no one in his family would have guessed, since he was the most cooperative sibling. After praying and sharing his struggles with God, Wayne chose to surrender these impulses, releasing his sexual tension into God's care. This surrender became a daily practice, guiding him as he learned to submit his growing sexuality to God.

Biblical Example

Now Joseph was well-built and handsome, 7 and after a while his master's wife took notice of Joseph and said, "Come to bed with me!"

8 But he refused. "With me in charge," he told her, "my master does not concern himself with anything in the house; everything he owns he has entrusted to my care. 9 No one is greater in this house than I am. My master has withheld nothing from me except you, because you are his wife. How then could I do such a wicked thing and sin

against God?" [10] And though she spoke to Joseph day after day, he refused to go to bed with her or even be with her.

[11] One day he went into the house to attend to his duties, and none of the household servants was inside. [12] She caught him by his cloak and said, "Come to bed with me!" But he left his cloak in her hand and ran out of the house. (Genesis 39:7-12)

Where Generation Alpha Is Now When It Comes to Surrender

Research on Generation Alpha suggests they are developing characteristics that point toward a low propensity to "surrender" in traditional terms, favoring independence, critical thinking, and questioning authority. They are raised in environments that foster personal agency and encourage them to challenge norms.

Key traits relevant to the concept of surrender include:

- **Challenging Authority:** Unlike previous generations, Generation Alpha is more likely to ask "Why?" and question established norms.
- **Independence and Self-Reliance:** Growing up with constant access to information has fostered strong self-awareness. They are encouraged to be entrepreneurial and self-directed, often preferring control over their future rather than yielding to external structures.
- **Focus on Resilience, Not Submission:** Values such as grit and bouncing back from challenges are emphasized, particularly in response to global events like the COVID-19 pandemic. Parents and educators encourage learning from failure, focusing on resilience rather than surrender.
- **Social Consciousness and Agency:** Generation Alpha is highly aware of social issues and feels empowered to create change. This desire to actively shape their world reflects

a proactive approach rather than passive surrender to circumstances.

Overall, Generation Alpha is a generation with a strong voice and a proactive approach to life, less likely to surrender by default and more inclined to seek understanding, assert their needs, and carve their own path. Teaching surrender in the context of sexuality requires showing them that submitting their desires to God is not weakness but an empowered choice that leads to integrity, self-control, and a life that honors Christ.

How Generation Alpha Can Benefit from Biblical Surrender

Generation Alpha can gain deeply from learning and practicing biblical surrender, which teaches trust in God and letting go of the need to control every outcome. In today's world, where information is instant, social media pressures are constant, and change feels relentless, developing spiritual resilience is more important than ever. Practicing surrender can help young people manage anxiety and the mental health challenges common in their generation, offering a sense of peace and security rooted in the understanding that their lives have meaning beyond immediate concerns. This practice nurtures humility, patience, and reliance on faith, qualities that create a stable foundation in the face of life's often chaotic and competitive demands.

Beyond personal stability, biblical surrender encourages Alpha youth to focus on relational values rather than individual success or digital recognition. By yielding personal ambitions to God's will, they can cultivate empathy, compassion, and a stronger sense of community. This approach helps counter the isolation that often comes with heavy digital engagement, promoting selflessness and service toward others. Ultimately, surrender equips Generation Alpha to navigate complex ethical situations with integrity and grace, fostering a generation grounded in faith, inner strength, and moral clarity, better prepared to meet future challenges with wisdom and resilience.

Signs to Engage Practice with Youth

- Youth exhibit anxiety or stress when outcomes feel out of their control.
- They struggle with perfectionism or excessive self-reliance.
- Teens often prioritize digital or personal achievement over community or relational values.
- They resist guidance or have difficulty yielding in challenging situations.
- They express frustration, impatience, or impulsivity in moral or relational decisions.
- They show a desire for inner peace, meaning, or guidance, but struggle to find it.

Supporting Scriptures

- Matthew 16:24
- James 4:7
- Proverbs 23:26
- Romans 12:2
- 2 Timothy 2:22

Steps to Engage Surrender as a Practice with Youth

1. Select a given struggle.
2. Identify stories of surrender and supporting Scriptures as listed above.
3. Discuss the steps taken in Scripture that led to surrender.
4. Discuss the struggle in raw detail.

5. Discuss ways that steps can be taken toward surrender. Support the youth until they are able to fully surrender the struggle.

Practice 2: Socratic Conversations

Socratic conversations are a great way to help kids really connect with Scripture and make it their own. Instead of just being told what to believe, they get to ask questions, think things through, and talk openly about what they're learning. When they have a safe space to explore, they can wrestle with tricky ideas, understand people's motives, and grow closer to God while figuring things out for themselves.

Real-Life Example

Miranda sat in a circle with her peers after reading the book of Ezra at the tender age of ten. But even today, as an eighteen-year-old, she remembers how transformative the experience was. While many of her friends drifted away from faith, Miranda stayed rooted. They freely discussed the Israelites' command to leave their ungodly wives who worshiped idols. With prompt after prompt from her Sunday school teacher— "What would you have done?" "Why do you think this command was given?" "How do you think the husbands felt?"—Miranda found herself diving deeper into Scripture. She reflected on her own experiences and applied the lessons to her life. It wasn't about being told what to believe; it was about owning her faith. Through these conversations, Miranda came to know God intimately. Her understanding of Scripture became personal and transformative, shaping her life in ways no external influence could shake.

As she encountered sexual battles in life, she applied Socratic conversations with close friends and even with God. She learned how to skillfully take every thought captive and make it obedient to Christ.

Biblical Example

Jesus often engaged in question-and-answer dialogue to teach and reveal deeper truths:

- "Why were you searching for me?" (Luke 2:49)
- "Didn't you know I was about my Father's business?" (Luke 2:49)
- "Where are your accusers?" (John 8:10)
- "Who do people say that I am?" (Matthew 16:13)

These questions exemplify the Socratic approach: probing, reflective, and aimed at deeper insight. The method, originating with the ancient Greek philosopher Socrates (470–399 BCE), used questioning to expose contradictions and explore complex ideas. Jesus modeled this approach both as a youth in the temple and later in His ministry, guiding others toward understanding and revealing hidden motives.

The Bereans in Acts also modeled Socratic conversations, examining the Scriptures daily to verify Paul's teachings. They questioned, reflected, and debated until they confirmed that Christ was indeed their Lord and Savior. This same style of learning is reflected in modern education through the work of Mortimer Adler, a philosopher and educator who helped develop the Paideia Project, an educational model focused on teaching students how to think critically, read deeply, and engage ideas through discussion and inquiry. The Paideia Project similarly uses Socratic methods to help students read, research, and develop in-depth academic and analytical skills.

Allowing children to explore Scripture through inquiry helps them take ownership of their understanding. Socratic conversations provide the freedom to ask hard questions, wrestle with complex ideas, and build a personal, resilient faith. This practice mirrors how ancient rabbis taught, reflects Jesus' own method of teaching, and equips youth to internalize truth while developing critical thinking skills and a deep love for God's Word.

Where Generation Alpha Is with Socratic Conversations

Generation Alpha kids are growing up fully in the digital world, so most of their communication happens through screens—texting, video calls, and social media—rather than long face-to-face conversations. Because of that, they don't always get a lot of practice in deep, back-and-forth discussions like Socratic conversations. Some studies even suggest this can make it harder for them to focus for long stretches or think critically in structured ways. That said, they are naturally curious and love to explore ideas—but usually in a fast, hands-on style. So, while they might struggle with traditional Socratic dialogue in classrooms, they still have the potential to benefit if given the right space and guidance.

How Generation Alpha Can Benefit from Socratic Conversations

When kids engage in face-to-face Socratic conversations with peers, adults, or people from different backgrounds, it gives them skills they can't get online. This kind of discussion helps them think deeply, reflect on their own ideas, and learn to ask the right questions. It also teaches empathy and understanding, because they hear different perspectives and learn to explain their own thoughts clearly—without relying on social media filters. By balancing screen time with real-life dialogue, kids can strengthen their social skills, manage stress better, and build resilience. These are skills that will help them navigate a complex, fast-changing world and grow into adults who can think critically, care deeply, and communicate effectively.

Signs To Engage Socratic Conversations as a Practice with Youth

- Kids ask lots of questions and show curiosity about moral, spiritual, or life issues.
- They are willing to discuss ideas but don't always know how to articulate them.
- They show interest in exploring the *"why"* behind rules, teachings, or beliefs.
- They enjoy debating, sharing opinions, or hearing different viewpoints.
- They seem frustrated when given answers without explanation or when discussions are one-sided.
- They are open to reflecting on their own experiences and linking them to broader lessons.
- They get excited when conversations allow them to discover insights rather than just being told what to believe.

Supporting Scripture

- Acts 17:2-3
- Luke 12:27-28
- Job 38:1-14
- Proverbs 25:2

Steps to Engaging in Socratic Conversation as a Practice

1. Select a portion of Scripture on a given topic
2. Identify the basics of who, what, when, where, why, and how of the given text
3. Prompt students with questions like: Why do you think ...? What would you do in this situation? Put yourself in their shoes, how would you describe the way you would feel?

4. Have students read the text and ask raw, unedited questions about the text.
5. Respond to questions vulnerably and honestly based on Scripture.
6. When you do not have answers, be honest and say so.
7. Add time to research Scripture for difficult questions.

Practice 3: Intergenerational Small Groups

Intergenerational small groups are a powerful way to build faith, character, and emotional resilience. These groups bring together youth, peers, and adults, creating spaces where stories, wisdom, and encouragement flow across generations. When young people hear the lived experiences of older members and are invited to share their own struggles, they gain perspective, connection, and a sense of belonging that's hard to replicate in peer-only environments or online communities.

Real-Life Example

Rashauna couldn't believe her ears as she sat in a small group made up of four friends her age, two older teens, and three adults (two men and one woman).

One of the women shared her life story, from struggling with multiple sexual relationships as a teen to the day the Lord began to set her free. She spoke openly, in detail, and she felt her ears widen, her mouth drop, and her heart fill with compassion and safety. Rashauna noticed how no one judged her or threw stones; instead, one of the adults prayed over her as she recounted her journey.

That was the moment Rashauna realized she could bring her own struggles into this space without fear. It was a place she wanted to be part of—and a place she wanted her friends to experience.

Many adults underestimate what young people go through, but sitting there, Rashauna understood how meaningful guidance and empathy could bridge that gap. Rashauna felt hopeful that even with the inappropriate sexual behaviors in her life, she could begin the journey of surrendering this part of her life to Christ.

Biblical Example

These commandments that I give you today are to be on your hearts. Impress them on your children. Talk about them when you sit at home and when you walk along the road, when you lie down and when you get up. Tie them as symbols on your hands and bind them on your foreheads. Write them on the doorframes of your houses and on your gates. (Deuteronomy 6:6–9)

The transfer of spiritual truths to our children is one that God established long before youth ministries became modernized. The means was through multigenerational members of God's family. The older was to practice passing the baton via modeling and apprenticeship of what it looked like to trust and walk according to God's precepts.

Where Generation Alpha Stands with Intergenerational Small Groups

Generation Alpha, the first generation to grow up fully digital, often has limited interaction with people outside their immediate circles. Much of their communication happens online or through curated social spaces, and many rely heavily on parents or tech for guidance during their formative years. While this tech-savvy upbringing gives them strong digital skills, it often comes at the expense of real face-to-face interaction. This can make social communication harder, create feelings of isolation, and limit their ability to navigate real-time conflicts or problem-solve with others. Emotionally and mentally, a lack of authentic, in-person community can contribute to higher rates of anxiety, loneliness, and even depression. Spiritually, Generation Alpha may struggle to connect with traditional faith communities in meaningful ways, as much of their exposure is virtual and intermittent. This can mean missing out on the deeper, long-lasting faith formation that comes from intentional, multi-generational relationships.

How Engaging in Intergenerational Small Groups Can Benefit Generation Alpha

Bringing Generation Alpha into Bible-based intergenerational small groups can make a real difference. These groups create spaces where young people connect with older believers, share experiences, and receive guidance without fear of judgment. This helps them build a strong sense of identity that isn't tied solely to peers or online trends, but grounded in their God-given value and dignity. Socially and emotionally, these groups provide face-to-face connection, helping youth develop empathy, emotional regulation, and other critical social skills while counteracting digital isolation. Spiritually, they offer a safe place to ask questions, explore their faith, and gain wisdom from compassionate mentors on topics like relationships, sexuality, and moral choices. In short, intergenerational groups give Generation Alpha a sense of belonging, stability, and guidance that aligns with their search for authenticity and meaning in a fast-changing world.

Supporting Scriptures

- Luke 10:38
- Hebrews 10:25
- Ecclesiastes 4:9-10

Steps to Engage Intergenerational Small Groups as a Practice with Youth

1. Select safe, mature Christian adults who have overcome in the given area of concern (e.g. anger. sadness, sexual sin, or temptation, etc.).
2. Select a time and safe space to get together for a particular concern.
3. Create a series of Scriptures to be read from the list of reference sheets on the topic.
4. Have the adult prepare an age-appropriate sharing of their testimony to share with the child.
5. Have them share it with the child.
6. Allow the child to respond to what meant the most to them from what they heard from the trusted adult.
7. Provide time for the child to share their struggle.
8. Include a related Scripture for them to meditate on for the week and for further discussion for a follow-up time together.

Practice 4: Worship

Worship is more than just singing songs, it's actually a way for young people to connect with God, express their hearts, and find freedom and peace. For Generation Alpha who is growing up in a fast-paced, hyper-digital world, worship can be a grounding practice that helps them slow down, process their emotions, and experience God personally. When approached intentionally, worship allows them to move beyond just hearing words or melodies to actually encountering God and seeing His presence shape their thoughts, decisions, and identity.

Real-Life Example

Krissy found herself trapped in a relationship with her boyfriend. It wasn't just sexual, it was emotional too, and she had no idea how to break free.

He had become her whole world, but he had other girlfriends, tearing her apart inside. Nobody knew the extent of what was happening, not even her friends. Her mind was a war zone, and she struggled to know how to silence it.

As she walked from the bus stop on her way home, listening to a worship song through her earphones that said, "My mind, my heart, my soul belongs to you," she realized none of it was true. Her heart, mind, and soul belonged to someone who didn't truly care for her.

Tears streamed down her face as she talked to God, desperate for help. Then, she heard the gentle voice of the Holy Spirit: "Krissy, I love you. I will help you." In that moment, she felt God's presence and began the first steps of release from a relationship that had felt impossible to leave.

Through worship, Krissy slowly learned to surrender her heart and reclaim her identity in God, experiencing freedom and hope she hadn't thought possible.

Where Is Generation Alpha When It Comes to Music and Worship?

Generation Alpha engages heavily with digital music. Streaming services dominate their listening habits, yet surprisingly, many still show interest in physical formats like CDs. Nearly 46 percent in one UK study, are seeking a sense of authenticity. However, their hyper-digital lives are strongly linked to rising anxiety, identity struggles, and social pressures. Constant online exposure, influencer trends, and the curated perfection seen on social media can disrupt traditional identity formation and leave young people feeling unmoored. The combination of these pressures with a lack of deep, intentional reflection can make it difficult for them to navigate their emotions, form a stable sense of self, or experience lasting mental and spiritual grounding.

In contrast, authentic worship offers enormous benefits. It provides belonging, reduces anxiety, and builds resilience through shared spiritual experiences. Music, especially worship music, interacts with the brain in ways that promote calm, focus, and emotional regulation. It helps youth process difficult emotions and experiences while creating space for God to speak into their lives. Worship allows them to step away from the pressures of digital culture and the isolation that can come with it, giving them a safe environment to reconnect with God and with themselves. By singing, listening, reflecting, and engaging fully, they can experience God's presence in a tangible way that grounds their identity, nurtures emotional and spiritual resilience, and cultivates hope.

For Generation Alpha, worship is not simply a passive activity; it's an active, transformative practice. It helps them reclaim control over their hearts and minds in a world that often feels overwhelming, provides a counterbalance to the negative pressures of social media and online life, and gives them a foundation to navigate both the joys and challenges of growing up. Through worship, they are invited to encounter God's love directly, release burdens, and build a sense of spiritual, emotional, and mental wellness that will equip them for a lifetime.

How Worship Can Benefit Generation Alpha

Worship gives the Generation Alpha an essential grounding in a world that's fast, complicated, and often overwhelming. It offers hope, a sense of identity, and moral clarity amid the constant pressures of social media, digital culture, and global events. When children engage in worship from an early age, they develop a spiritual foundation that anchors them and helps them feel connected to a larger community of believers. As Christian author John Ortberg explains, *"I need to worship because without it I can forget that I have a big God beside me and live in fear. I need to worship because without it I can forget his calling and begin to live in a spirit of self-preoccupation."*[20] Worship reminds young people that they are part of something bigger than themselves, helping counter the anxieties and self-focus that can dominate a generation growing up amidst global crises and constant digital exposure.

Beyond grounding, worship offers a powerful avenue for connecting with God's presence, receiving spiritual direction, and experiencing transformation that shapes character and purpose. When children observe adults engaged in sincere praise, prayer, and listening to God's Word, they learn how to express their own thoughts, fears, and hopes. This practice fosters a deep, personal faith that goes beyond routine or habit. Bob Kauflin, a noted author on worship, puts it beautifully: *"Worship changes the worshiper into the image of the One worshiped."*[21] For the Generation Alpha, this transformative power helps them align their lives with God's will, discover a hopeful purpose, and actively contribute to the life and mission of the church across generations.

Supporting Scriptures

- Zephaniah 3:17
- John 4:24
- Psalm 96:9

---

[20] John Ortberg — The Life You've Always Wanted: Spiritual Disciplines for Ordinary People (Zondervan, 1997), p. 108.
[21] (Kauflin, 2008, *Worship Matters*, p. 44)

- James 5:16
- Psalm 32:5
- 1 John 1:9

Steps to Engage Worship as a Practice with Youth

1. Get the child to quiet his/her heart, mind, and spirit down.
2. Have the child reflect on three to five things they value most about God.
3. Have the child share how God helped them in the given week.
4. Select songs that speak of the attributes of God and thanksgiving toward Him.
5. Spend time singing those songs until deeper engagement and response takes place from the child, like immersion in worship, tears, focus, or abandonment from distraction.
6. Close in prayer with the child and have them share what they got most from worshipping God.

Chapter 13

The Cries of Our Children-God's and Mine

The thirty years I have spent in the classroom have given me something that cannot compare to the research I read regularly about them. As the old saying goes, you can't make this stuff up. In many ways, I have become a student before my students in learning about them, their needs, and their cries. For years, I would spend hours crying over their cries, praying for God's interventions over their lives. I'd love to say that much of my experience came from the church, but in actuality, it was through being in inner-city public schools that I was able to engage with the unedited versions of children and their families. I got to see representations of our public as it relates to what God says when He says, "Go into the highways and byways," Luke 14:23.

Because I work with children, I often grow close to their parents and have often been permitted to journey with them, cry with them, and pray with them. As a parent myself, I feel tenderness and sensitivity when it comes to my students and their parents and relatives. We are partners in providing opportunities to allow children to become the best versions of who they have been called to be.

Throughout my time in prayer over the years, God would give me these dreams that, for a long time, I did not think much of; but as I faced the latter part of my years, I began to feel the irony of Him giving me so many dreams that not only included me but also included children within the age group that I teach. A few messages and revelations that stand out the most about what God has spoken to my heart are to begin giving our Generation Alpha, the youngest in our population, the raw and unedited Word of God in full context, allowing them to compare Scripture to Scripture. This allows them to solidify their faith.

Another strong message is to provide opportunities for them to take ownership of their faith. Instead of monologue sessions, let's provide a dialogue as seen in my dream in Section One. This generation has enough verbiage to ask hard questions and be provided with profound answers if we allow the space. This example is seen with Jesus as a youth and with the Bereans. It is a model that we should not ignore. Freedom to discuss, scaffold, and analyze Scripture should be the norm. I have had great opportunities to witness the greatness that comes from friends like Heidi Heiderich, a youth Bible teacher in Asheville, North Carolina. It is also what God is challenging me to do in this next chapter in my life. The details related to this have not yet been unfolded, but I fear God too much not to seek Him with all of my heart to find out how.

One day, I heard God's voice echo in my heart saying, "Why is it that the youth know so much about David and Goliath and not anything about David and Bathsheba?" He told me to stop providing only parts of His Word to His children and to give them all of it, especially as it relates to sexuality. It's no wonder that the last place our youth go is to the church and trusted spiritual adults about their questions related to sex. We should be approachable and provide safe spaces for such conversations.

Sadly, I have seen kids tormented with voices they hear in their heads and overcome with anxiety and pain that the average adult could hardly bear to carry. All of these are cries for us to grow in our spiritual maturity and look into providing spiritual apprenticeship for our youth. We have enough godly adults that if each Christian church paired an adult with one child, our children can be greatly nourished in Christ and protected from a culture that seeks to sift them like wheat.

Practices are God's response in providing tangible ways that bridge children from where they are with the help of the Holy Spirit to where God is. We can shift them from being the generation known as the digital, hypersexualized, and anxious to one that grows so in love with Christ that we provoke the rest of the world to jealousy when they see the joy infused within the lives of our children. We do not know if Generation Alpha will be the generation that will see the Lord, but we can train them so that if their kids are, they will be strongly equipped to win every battle the enemy throws at them.

For more than thirty years I have stood in two classrooms.

One classroom had rows of desks, fluorescent lights, and the restless energy of children growing up in the noise of the modern world. The other classroom had wooden pews, open Bibles, and the quiet longing of young hearts searching for God. One was an inner-city public school. The other was a Sunday school.

In both places I have listened carefully to the voices of children.

And in recent years, those voices have been crying out.

Not always with words—but with anxiety, confusion, exhaustion, and a quiet ache for identity.

This book was born from those cries.

A Generation Carrying More Than They Should

The children being raised today—often called Generation Alpha—are growing up in a world unlike any generation before them.

They are the first generation raised almost entirely in a digital world. Before they understand who they are, algorithms are already shaping their identity. Before they learn to sit quietly with their thoughts, endless streams of information are competing for their attention.

Many of them spend hours every day on social media, absorbing voices that tell them who they should be, what they should desire, and how they should define themselves. And the result I have witnessed again and again in my classrooms is heartbreaking:

Children who are anxious before they are teenagers.

Children who are confused about identity before they even understand adulthood.

Children who feel alone in rooms full of people.

I have watched students wrestle with overwhelming anxiety. I have sat with young people confused about who they are. I have listened to stories of isolation, comparison, pressure, and silent despair.

These are not statistics to me.

These are children whose faces I remember.

Some of their stories appear in this book.

And they are crying out for help.

A Surprising Discovery in an Ancient Faith

As a teacher, I spent years asking a simple question:

How do we help this generation not just survive—but become whole?

The answer did not come from modern strategies or digital solutions.

It came from something far older.

It came from the life of Jesus.

When I began studying the early life and practices of Jesus more deeply, something profound emerged. Jesus also lived in a complicated world filled with pressure, expectations, and confusion. Yet the Gospels show a young man who possessed clarity, peace, wisdom, and deep connection with God.

This did not happen by accident.

Jesus lived a life rooted in ancient spiritual practices that shaped His mind, His identity, and His relationship with His Heavenly Father.

These practices were not rituals without purpose. They were living bridges between earth and heaven.

They grounded the human heart in the presence of an invisible God.

And they formed the inner life of Jesus long before His public ministry began.

What I discovered is that these same practices—if lived intentionally—can anchor the hearts of our children.

Closing Reflections – The Practice

Ancient Practices for a Modern Storm

This book is not simply about diagnosing the struggles of Generation Alpha.

It is about guiding families toward practices that form resilient, faith-filled young hearts:

Practices that Jesus Himself lived.

Practices that shaped the disciples.

Practices that sustained believers for thousands of years.

Throughout these pages I introduce parents and families to powerful rhythms such as:

- **Biblical meditation** that quiets the anxious mind and roots identity in God's truth
- **Epistle writing** that teaches children to process their thoughts, prayers, and struggles honestly before God
- **Reflection and journaling** that helps young people recognize God's work in their daily lives
- **Studying Scripture in its full context**, not as fragments but as a living story of God's relationship with humanity

- **Socratic conversations** that invite children to ask deep questions and seek wisdom rather than shallow answers
- **Worship** that reorients the heart toward God's presence
- **Sabbath and rest**, which interrupt the relentless noise of the digital world

These are not outdated religious habits.

They are soul-forming practices.

They are pathways that help young people encounter God personally rather than merely hear about Him.

And they cultivate something every parent longs for:

A faith that is not borrowed—but owned.

Stories from the Front Lines

Over three decades of teaching, I have watched the cultural landscape change dramatically. I have seen the rise of smartphones, social media, and digital identities.

But I have also seen something else.

I have seen what happens when young people experience God through intentional spiritual practices.

In this book, I share real stories from students I have encountered along the way—young people navigating anxiety, identity confusion, family struggles, and deep questions about life.

Some of these moments happened in classrooms.

Some happened in church hallways.

Some happened during quiet conversations after lessons had ended.

These stories reveal both the wounds of this generation, and the incredible resilience God has placed within them.

They also reveal something that has deeply shaped my own faith journey: the mysterious ways God still speaks.

At times in my life, God has spoken through dreams and encounters that carried powerful messages about the condition of this generation and the hope that remains for them. Those experiences became moments of awakening for me—reminding me that God sees these children, hears their struggles, and has not abandoned them to navigate this confusing world alone.

A Call to Parents and Godly Guardians

If you are a parent or guardian reading this summary, I want you to hear this clearly:

Your child's faith cannot survive on Sunday mornings alone.

The world discipling your children operates twenty-four hours a day.

Their phones preach messages.

Their peers preach messages.

Social media preaches messages.

But the good news is that God has already given us an apprenticeship framework that has shaped hearts for thousands of years.

The practices Jesus lived are not reserved for ancient times.

They are meant for families today.

When these practices become part of the rhythm of your home, something powerful begins to happen.

Children learn to slow down.

They learn to listen.

They learn to wrestle with truth rather than run from it.

They begin to recognize the voice of God.

And slowly—sometimes quietly, sometimes dramatically—their identity becomes anchored in something far stronger than culture.

Bridging Earth and Heaven

One of the greatest challenges for young believers today is the feeling that God is distant or invisible.

The ancient practices described in this book bridge that gap.

They teach children how to live in awareness of God's presence.

They create space for God to speak into anxious minds.

They nurture spiritual attentiveness in a distracted generation.

And they remind us that faith was never meant to be passive.

It was always meant to be practiced.

Jesus did not merely teach spiritual truth.

He lived it daily—and invited His disciples to do the same.

This book invites parents to guide their children into that same apprenticeship.

A Hopeful Future

Despite the struggles I have witnessed over three decades, I remain deeply hopeful.

I believe Generation Alpha has enormous potential.

I believe they are capable of deep faith, courageous leadership, and spiritual wisdom.

But they will need parents who are willing to lead them into a different rhythm than the culture around them:

Parents who are willing to slow down. Parents who are willing to ask deeper questions. Parents who are willing to practice the ancient ways of faith inside their homes.

This book is my invitation to you:

An invitation to rediscover practices that formed the hearts of believers for centuries. An invitation to walk beside your children as they encounter the living God. And an invitation to believe that even in the confusion of this modern age, God is still calling young hearts to Himself.

I have seen the struggles of this generation. But I have also seen the power of God at work in their lives.

And I believe that when families return to the ancient paths that Jesus walked, a generation searching for identity will finally discover who they were created to be.

As we come to a close...

I thank God for the grace and honor to partner with Him in this work with children, their parents, and godly leaders. This book has been a burden on my heart for so many years and was at risk to not happen at all. The actual writings took place in the midnight hours of the small time I had after long working hours, but its impressions marinated on my heartstrings daily and for years as I walked, talked, and served children. Their academics slowly became lesser shadows and the needs of their souls and spirits became more evident and an even higher priority. We know that the entrance of God's Word brings forth light; therefore, when the spirit of a child is enlightened by God's truth, all other areas are freed to flourish.

Our kids are in need of being rescued from the entanglements of this world and we are the ones that must grow spiritually and be able to rescue and free them. We must pull them away from the darkness that crouches at the door in wait just to consume them, to consume who they are as they are made in His image, to consume the inheritance given to us through them. This is a serious call. It is a serious cry.

We have more to put our hands to than words can express and this book only touches the surface. The effectual fervent prayers of the righteous availeth much and we must stand in the gap and cry out loud for the sake of our children. Can you feel the spiritual hunger pangs of our children? Do you cry as you think of their vulnerable disposition? If you do, I am asking that you will begin committing a child in your life to prayer and even some of these practices. Can you put a letter in the mail? Can you invite them to lunch? Can you cultivate a profound question that would leave them to dig for answers for an eternity until they latch arms with the Father? Whatever you do, do not cast a blind eye to what may be happening to the inner man of the child in your community. They may be in your neighborhood, a niece or nephew. They may be your grandchild, your best friend's child, or in your Sunday school.

Honestly, before I began my thirty-year journey as a teacher, my only desire was to stay home and give my own children all the love stored in my heart from God, yet that prayer never came to fruition. The Lord provided me with a front-row seat to not only my own children but to children in the public squares of life, children from the highways and byways, and it gave me a picture outside of myself, outside of my personal worldview and into His point of view. He said, "Tamara, I know your deepest desire is to have the best interest of your own children, but would you join Me in peering into the world of the children I see every day?" He said, "Tamara, can you co-labor with Me on this journey so that I can teach you something as you teach My children?" I hesitantly said, "I guess." I ended up falling in love with the children I serve daily. I saw into their hearts, their longings, and above all their cries. The burden for them has not been easy. Doing things that were out of the box as a Christian teacher in the public sector was often welcomed by some but ostracized by many, but I was confident that God walked and journeyed with me throughout all of my teaching journey. He gave me silly songs in the night to sing to them in the mornings. He told me to have compassion where a referral was warranted. He told me to laugh with them and tell jokes that would break the coldness in their abandoned hearts.

For my own children, ancient biblical practices were interwoven into our tight working schedule and served as a bridge to the close and intimate relationship I share with each child today and how they commune with God. From letter writing to long walks and talks, from doing communion in the home to long drives of reflections. They are practices that helped me to point them to our Father in heaven. It has not been perfect, but the effect of practices in our home has been permanent as my children embark upon becoming young adults and get to know God for themselves. We are definitely in an era of information, but what our children are more in need of is encounters (based on Scripture) that will never erase from the crevices of their souls and spirits.

I am enamored by the journey of serving children, yet I would be lying if I did not express my level of exhaustion in carrying so many of their spiritual, emotional, and academic burdens. This is certainly an assignment I could never manufacture on my own and one that is focused on the youngest part of our population

— the Generation Alpha. It is an assignment that stares us square in the face every day and an assignment that God is calling for each member of the body of Christ to join in as a stakeholder. We can serve in small ways, big ways, but we must put our hands to the plow in some way.

I pray that as you have joined me in this small peek into the world of our Generation Alpha that your heart has been stirred to at least pray on how you can invest in our children by responding to their cry. Please join me in prayer.

> *Father,*
>
> *You have journeyed with us as we've visited the heart-wrenching cries of our youngest, the Generation Alpha.*
>
> *You sent Your only begotten Son to experience all the cries that children today experience. He was ostracized, bullied, dehumanized, and belittled, and He cried out at the deepest core of His being. For this reason, He is not only able to identify with the cries of our children, but they can come to identify with Him as their Lord and Savior.*
>
> *Your Son Jesus is closely acquainted with the cries of our children, and we present our children to You. We present their quiet and deepest cries to You, and we ask that You deepen our faith and understanding of who You are in order to guide them in walking in a more meaningful way with You.*
>
> *In the world we live in, there is no other answer. You are the only answer we have, and so we fix our eyes on You. Show us how to walk and talk and journey with our children according to their spiritual design, and may You create lasting impressions that will cause them to always revisit those memories even when they have been tempted to abandon their faith.*

May their encounters with You be of greater value to their beings than what the world offers them. Because You joined our children in their pain, because You saw into the heart of a child while You suffered as a child, carrying all the sins of the world and then overcoming them through Your sacrifice on the cross, we know that all of these requests are possible for any child we lay our eyes on and bring to You in prayer and service.

Amen.

Bibliography

Barna, George. *Transforming Children into Spiritual Champions: Why Children Should Be Your Church's #1 Priority*. Grand Rapids, Michigan, Baker Books, A Division of Baker Publishing Group, 2016.

Bowman, Matt, and Isaac Morehouse. *Open Education*. Elite Online Publishing, 1 Apr. 2025.

Chen, Ying, and Tyler J VanderWeele. "Chen and VanderWeele Respond to "Religion, Spirituality, and Health."" *American Journal of Epidemiology*, vol. 189, no. 8, 4 Mar. 2020, pp. 759–760, https://doi.org/10.1093/aje/kwaa021. Accessed 10 Apr. 2021.

Coles, Robert. *The Mind's Fate*. 1 Sept. 1975.

Cunningham, Loren. *Making Jesus Lord: The Dynamic Power of Laying down Your Rights*. WASHINGTON, SEATTLE, YWAM PUBLISHING, 1988.

Genspect. "My Daughter's School Transitioned Her without Telling Me - January Littlejohn." *YouTube*, 27 Jan. 2024, www.youtube.com/watch?v=wCshcfx4CSc. Accessed 15 May 2025.

John Mark Comer. *Practicing the Way*. Colorado Springs, WaterBrook, 16 Jan. 2024.

Kinnaman, David, and Mark Matlock. Faith for Exiles: 5 Ways for a New Generation to Follow Jesus in Digital Babylon. Grand Rapids, Mi, Baker Books, 2019.

Mittelstadt, Martin W. "Misreading Scripture with Western Eyes: Removing Cultural Blinders to Better Understand the Bible. By E. Randolph Richards and Brandon J. O'Brien. Downers Grove, IL: Inter Varsity Press, 2012. Pp. 240. $16.00." *Religious Studies Review*, vol. 39, no. 2, June 2013, pp. 88–88, https://doi.org/10.1111/rsr.12029_32. Accessed 1 Mar. 2021.

Mulvihill, Josh. Grandparenting: Strengthening Your Family and Passing on Your Faith. Grand Rapids, Bethany House Publishers, 2018.

Pastor Allen Nolan. "Childhood of Jesus | the Silent Years of Jesus Bible Study | Pastor Allen Nolan Sermon." *YouTube*,. 3 Oct. 2018, www.youtube.com/watch?v=z3prHMjY11M. Accessed 1 Mar. 2026.

Paul David Tripp. *Sex in a Broken World*. Crossway, 16 Jan. 2018.

Stucky, Nathan T. *Wrestling with Rest: Inviting Youth to Discover the Gift of Sabbath*. Grand Rapids, Michigan, William B. Eerdmans Publishing Company, 2019.

About the Author

Dr. **Tamara Denis-Lewis** is a first-generation Haitian American, seasoned educator, and author with over 30 years of experience teaching in inner-city schools. She holds a Bachelor's degree in English Literature from Florida International University, a Master of Arts in Education from Regent University, and a Doctorate in Ministry from North Greenville University. A recipient of numerous district awards for her excellence in academic instruction, Dr. Denis-Lewis brings a deeply informed and compassionate perspective to her work.

Throughout her decades-long teaching career and years serving in youth ministry, Dr. Denis-Lewis has closely observed the growing spiritual and emotional crisis affecting today's youngest generation, those in the Alpha age group. Deeply concerned by their struggles with identity, emotional trauma, and sexual confusion, she has devoted herself to prayer, study, and scriptural insight to address these issues from a biblical lens.

Her writing is shaped by personal experience, prophetic encounters, and academic research, culminating in her recent book, *The Cry*, where she offers hope and guidance to parents, clergy, and teachers navigating these challenges. Dr. Denis-Lewis writes with a nurturing voice and a mission to restore clarity, faith, and identity to a generation in need.